Learner's Guide to accompany

Principles of Instructional Design Third Edition

by
Walter W. Wager, Florida State University
James M. Applefield, University of North Carolina, Wilmington
Rodney S. Earle, University of North Carolina, Wilmington
John V. Dempsey, University of South Alabama

Harcourt Brace Jovanovich College Publishers
Fort Worth   Philadelphia   San Diego
New York   Orlando   Austin   San Antonio
Toronto   Montreal   London   Sydney   Tokyo

ISBN: 0-03-033982-0

PRINTED IN THE UNITED STATES OF AMERICA

2 3   017   9 8 7 6 5 4 3 2

Harcourt Brace Jovanovich, Inc.
The Dryden Press
Saunders College Publishing

Purpose:
This learner's guide was designed to accompany the text *Principles of Instructional Design*, by Robert M. Gagné, Leslie J. Briggs, and Walter W. Wager. Although originally planned as a student learner's guide for use in instructional design courses, others may also find it useful for self-study or in training situations.

Format:
Each chapter in the guide corresponds with a chapter text and contains the following:

1. An overview of the chapter.
2. Objectives for each of the chapters.
3. Practice exercises and feedback on verbal information and concept objectives.
4. Practical exercises related to higher-order skills
5. An extended set of examples for concepts and principles

Background:

In the text *Principles of Instructional Design*, Gagné, Briggs, and Wager develop an instructional design model based on a cognitive learning model. The text elaborates on four different technologies:

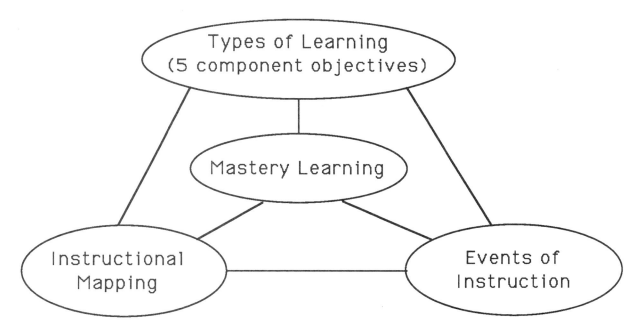

1. The classification of learned behaviors into different types of performance outcomes
2. Events of Instruction
3. Instructional Mapping
4. Mastery Learning

The Gagné, Briggs, Wager model of instructional design is internally consistent and easy to apply to a broad range of education and training situations. One may apply any of the different components

Preface

independent of the others, but it is most powerful when all are used together. The position taken by the authors of this learner's guide is that the information in the text will make more sense and be more meaningful if it is applied to your every-day instructional problems. The way to gain skill with the model is to practice applying it through the practice questions and the practical exercises contained in this learner's guide.

Using the Learner's Guide:

We suggest you read the overview and objectives in the learner's guide, read the chapter in the text, do the practice questions, and check your answers. The practical exercises can be used to check your ability to apply the information presented in the practice exercises. In some chapters we have included model answers for the practical exercises from students in our classes so that you might compare your work to theirs. In some chapters group activities and class discussions are recommended.

Finally, use the model to design your own course materials. We hope you will find it both challenging and rewarding.

Acknowledgments

The authors would like to acknowledge the contributions of their students in preparing this work-book. The workbook has been used in a variety of classes, and feedback from students has shaped the format and activities. We especially want to thank those students who allowed us to use their examples of the practical exercises. Thanks are also due to Diane Wilkes for her editorial assistance on early drafts. Finally, we wish to acknowledge Holt, Rinehart and Winston for experimenting with a publication prepared on a desktop publishing system.

A student guide is intended to help students in learning the principles and procedures contained in the textbook with which it is associated. This guide aims to accomplish such a purpose for the book *Principles of Instructional Design*, third edition. The authors are faculty members of three universities. In combination, they have had many years of experience in teaching the principles contained in the textbook, and in observing students' behavior as they undertake to gain understanding of the instructional design process.

A guide of this sort can be of inestimable help to students who aim to comprehend the principles of instructional design, and to incorporate them into personal skills. This guide begins with foundations in learning theory, and then goes on to deal with the procedures of instructional design in a practical sense. Chapters of the guide follow those of the basic text, from defining performance objectives through the selection of media to the techniques of student assessment and program evaluation.

The guide can help students in a number of ways. First of all, it provides a review of the material contained in the basic text, and an emphasis of its main ideas. The major concepts are related in a new context, thus supporting improved retention. Questions challenge the learner to retrieve what has been learned, and to use it in connection with newly presented statements. The transfer of knowledge is promoted by problem solving exercises. Student exercises keyed to each chapter of the text give many opportunities for review and application practice.

This work exemplifies the devotion to students' interests exhibited by the experienced instructors who have developed and tested out these helpful study activities. It may be confidently expected that as successive classes of students attain the high levels of skillfulness reflected by the exercises in this book, the field of instructional design will surely be enriched.

Robert M. Gagné
Tallahassee, Florida
October, 1989

Table of Contents

INTRODUCTION

Overview:

This chapter is an introduction to the concepts and terms that form the basis for the rest of the text. This includes some basic assumptions about instructional design, principles of learning, the learning process and the rationale for instructional design. For practice we suggest that you read the chapter and formulate questions about the assumptions being made. This could be followed by discussing the objectives or practice questions with others in a formal or informal setting. It should be possible to reach a consensus on the definitions as presented in the text.

Objectives:

1. **When asked, in the form of an oral or written question, state:**

    a) the differences between instruction and teaching

    b) a definition of "planned instruction "

    c) what a "systems approach" to instructional design means

    d) what the term "conditions of learning" means

    e) the purpose a model of learning serves in the design of instruction

    f) a definition of "events of instruction"

    g) the five types of learned capabilities and a brief description of each type

    h) why intellectual skills are considered the "building blocks of instruction"

    i) a summary, in your own words, of the philosophy reflected in a systems approach to instructional design, as presented by the authors in Chapter 1 of the text

Practice Exercises:

Answer the following questions which were derived from the objectives.

1 . a) Define instruction and teaching and discuss their differences.

b) What differentiates planned from unplanned instruction?

c) What is meant by the "systematic design" of instruction.

d) What is meant by the term "conditions of learning"?

e) What purpose does a model of learning serve in the design of instruction?

f) What are the "events of instruction" (don't list them)?

g) List the five types of learning outcomes and give a brief description of each type.

(1)

(2)

(3)

(4)

(5)

h) What are intellectual skills and in what way are they cumulative?
Why are intellectual skills considered building blocks?

Application Exercise:

The information in the first chapter forms the foundation for what will be presented in the rest of the text. One practical use of this information is to form a rationale for designing instruction in a systematic way, including considerations about the learning environment, the learner, and the type of learning outcome. Using this as a basis summarize, in your own words, the philosophy presented in Chapter 1 of the text.

Feedback for Practice Exercises:

1. a) Teaching is generally associated with lecture or tutoring, activities performed by the teacher. Instruction is generally considered broader than teaching and includes the arrangement of learning activities (events) that facilitate learning. These learning activities may be presented by a teacher or they may be mediated. In summary, teaching is one mode of instruction.

   b) Planned instruction considers the whole range of instructional events that facilitates learning. It is a guide for replicable (reliable) instruction, including learning aids, media, live instruction, and evaluation.

   c) A systems approach to instruction is a set of steps in designing instruction that includes analysis of the learning goals, task analysis, specification of the learning outcomes, and development of materials including trial and revision based on learner feedback (formative evaluation).

   d) The conditions of learning are all events, internal and external to the learner, that affect learning. Different types of learning require different conditions or events.

   e) A model attempts to show the relationships among the components of a system. A model of learning shows the components of the process called learning. A learning model is a convenient structure for formulating hypotheses about how external events of instruction affect internal information processing. The learning model used in the text is called a cognitive processing model, meaning that new learning is determined in large part by what the learner already knows, and the executive processes or learning strategies possessed by the learner.

   f) External events of instruction are a series of activities or instructional stimuli that facilitate internal information processing. The events presented in the text follow the stages in the information processing model.

   g) The five types of learning outcomes are:

       (1) Verbal information - labels, facts and organized knowledge

       (2) Intellectual skills - discriminations, concepts, rules, and problem solving

       (3) Cognitive strategies - learning strategies employed by the student

       (4) Attitudes - internal states that affect choice decisions

       (5) Motor skills - coordinated muscle movements

(h) Intellectual skills represent five different types of learning outcomes that build on each other in a cumulative manner. Intellectual skills are said to be "hierarchical" because each type of outcome is composed of skills from a lower level, e.g., concepts are composed of discriminations, rules are composed of concepts, problem solving involves the application of rules.

Criteria for Evaluating the Application Exercise:

Does the philosophy reflect three or more of the following?

1) That different types of learning outcomes require different types of instruction.

2) That planned instruction will be more effective than unplanned instruction.

3) That the systematic design of instruction requires consideration of the type of learning outcome desired and the skills possessed by the learner.

4) Learning is aimed at individuals. Instruction is oriented toward the individual even though it may be presented in group settings.

5) Designed instruction should be based on a model of how people learn. Instructional design must consider the conditions of learning necessary to ensure that the desired effects occur.

6) The systematic design of instruction involves a number of steps including the definition of desired learning outcomes, a strategy for obtaining those outcomes and evaluation to measure their attainment.

Example of a student answer to the application exercise by Jennifer Willis:

Chapter 1 asserts that instruction should be planned so as to maximize on both the internal and external condition which affect learning. To do so, it is possible to use a systematic approach which helps bring these factors into play, while allowing for differences that occur in terms of the learners and the content to be taught. In order to account for learner differences, the students or target audience should be understood before instruction is designed. Second, objectives should be formulated, with the emphasis on determining precisely what type of learning will take place. The type of learning, like the type of learner, has a direct impact on the type of instruction to be delivered.

Next, the systematic design process should begin to take into account the internal processes that are assumed to take place during learning. To affect these internal activities, the instruction should be structured, and activities devised, which reflect the various external events of instruction. Learning must also be traced back so that prerequisites are defined, either so they can be taught or so they can be reviewed and brought to the forefront of the learner's awareness before new learning takes place. This sequence is especially important for intellectual skills, which were discussed in their own section of the text. The hierarchical relationship of these various skills requires that they be learned in a precise order and the instruction must take this into account. Once this sequencing has been completed, learner assessment must be provided for and it should follow directly along the lines of the instructional objectives. In addition, assessment of the instruction is a critical factor.

Because of the number of variables already mentioned, there is room for error in designing instruction. Therefore, a good systematic approach will provide for a way to evaluate the course before, during, and after it is implemented with its target audience, and make revisions based on the evaluation. The use of a systematic approach guides the designer in dealing with these various issues and, hopefully, results in highly effective instruction.

DESIGNING INSTRUCTIONAL SYSTEMS

Overview:

Chapter 2 presents a systems approach model (a process) for planning instruction. The term "system" refers to an integration of parts that achieves a predetermined outcome. The outcome of an instructional design model is effective instruction.

This chapter introduces terminology derived from a systems view of instruction and presents a detailed discussion of a model in the form of a number of sequential steps in the design of instruction. While models of instructional design differ in certain respects, they all include components for analysis (and designation of learning outcomes), design (selecting appropriate instructional strategies), and evaluation of instruction. The Dick & Carey model is basically a nine-stage model that elaborates on these three fundamental "anchor points" of instructional design. The model shows that instructional design is an iterative process in that learner performance feedback is used to revise earlier decisions.

As you read the chapter, carefully consider the functions served by each stage of the model, and note their relationships to other stages. Also note the different types of instructional analysis. This model can guide your instructional design (ID) efforts and provide an advance organizer for the text. To fully comprehend the model, study the information and concepts related to each stage of the model and then complete the practice exercises. Use the practice exercises to review the information and conceptual base for the systematic ID model and its components. These exercises emphasize verbal information which is important in reading the remainder of the text.

We recommend that you complete ONE of the application exercises. This will give you an opportunity to outline the sequence of steps of the model in the context of a hypothetical design task.

Objectives:

1. When asked, in the form of an oral or written question, state

definitions of the following terms:
   a) instructional system
   b) instructional systems design
   c) instructional development
   d) instructional design
   e) instructional technology

   f) three generic functions found in any instructional systems model by listing them

   g) the 9 stages of the Dick & Carey instructional design (ID) model by reproducing a diagram of the model, putting all stages in proper sequence

   h) a brief (1-2 sentence) explanation of each of the 9 stages in the Dick & Carey ID model, in their order of occurrence

   i) three types of instructional analyses by listing the terms and explaining their purpose

j)   in your own words, three reasons for translating goal statements into performance objectives

k)   in your own words, four functions of performance objectives

l)   (1) the 'anchor points' in instructional design
      (2) a brief description of how they are related, including the rationale for designing tests before instruction

2. **When presented with an hypothetical design task and asked to describe the 9-step model as it would apply to that task, classify** each step, by citing an example of what would occur at that step.

Practice Exercises:

1. Define the following terms:
  a)   instructional system

  b)   instructional systems design

  c)   instructional development

  d)   instructional design

  e)   instructional technology.

  f)   What are the three common functions served by any instructional systems model? Categorize the nine stages into one of the three functions.

A_____   1._____

                                      2._____

                                      3._____

B_____   4._____

                                      5._____

                                      6._____

C_____   7._____

                                      8._____

                                      9._____

g) Reproduce the Dick & Carey ID model from memory.

h) Write a brief explanation of each step in the model above.

(1)

(2)

(3)

(4)

(5)

(6)

(7)

(8)

(9)

i) Define three types of instructional analysis and explain their purposes.

(1)

(2)

(3)

j) List three reasons for translating needs and goals into performance objectives.

(1)

(2)

(3)

k) List the four (4) functions that performance objectives serve.

(1)

(2)

(3)

(4)

I) (1) What are the three "anchor points" in planning and what is their desired relationship?

(a)

(b)

(c)

(2) List two reasons is it recommended that performance measures (tests) be designed prior to designing instructional strategies?

(a)

(b)

Application Exercises:

Complete one of the following exercises to help reinforce your understanding of the ID model presented in Chapter 2. Each of these exercises provides an opportunity to "apply" the model to a hypothetical design task. Note: Summative evaluation may not be practical for each of these tasks.

1. Consider a situation in which your training department supervisor has given you three months to develop a course for your company that will train managers to improve their skills in delegating responsibility, and increase the frequency of delegation. You have no specialized knowledge in the delegation of responsibility within an organization. However, you do have a good working understanding of a systems approach to instructional design; and there is an organizational behavior specialist working for the company. Using the nine-stage ID model, outline the steps that you would follow to design a training program to teach delegation skills.

2. Assume that after joining the Peace Corps, you are given a teaching assignment in a third world nation where English is not the first language of the people. Despite your urban background and history degree, you learn upon arrival in your host country that you are needed to help the government develop courses to teach community members how to operate and maintain an American-designed irrigation system.   Use the Dick & Carey model to systematically outline the steps for developing instruction to train technicians in a foreign setting.

3. Because of your college minor in creative arts, your principal has asked you to develop a drama curriculum for grades K-5 at your school. Although there is a curriculum guide for drama issued by the state, you have been given the latitude to create "your own program." Use the ID model of Dick & Carey to explain the process that you would follow in creating an elementary school drama curriculum.

Feedback for Practice Exercises:

1. a) instructional system - any organized effort to promote learning that specifies the learners, outcomes, resources and delivery procedures. They are readily observed at all school levels and in the training function in business and military settings.

   b) instructional systems design - a process of systematically planning instructional systems (all levels). It applies a systems approach (a generic problem solving strategy) for creating a comprehensive plan to facilitate learning.

   c) instructional development - refers to the implementation rather than the planning of an instructional system.

   d) instructional design - the planning of smaller systems of instruction such as courses, units or lessons.

   e) instructional technology - careful use of applicable theory to the design and development of instruction. Also refers to various means for promoting learning.

   f) The three (3) generic functions provided for in models of instructional systems design are: 1) specifying instructional outcomes; 2) designing the instruction; and 3) evaluating the results of the instruction. Stages 1-4 contribute to the identification of learning outcomes; stages 6 and 7 address the creation/selection of instructional strategies and materials; and stages 5, 8 and 9 are concerned with evaluation of learners' progress and the performance of the instructional system.

   g) See Figure 2-1, page 22 of Gagné, Briggs and Wager text for the Dick & Carey ID model.

   h) Stage 1. Identify Instructional Goals - Instructional goals are broad statements of the major learner outcomes that give initial, general direction to the planning of instruction. Goals are later analyzed into their constituent objectives.

   Stage 2. Conduct Instructional Analysis - Instructional analysis is the second (or third) stage in the ID model and provides a detailed specification of the learnings that comprise an instructional goal.

   Stage 3. Identify Entry Behaviors and Learner Characteristics - This stage requires analysis to determine which of the enabling skills (generally intellectual skills) learners bring to the learning task. Also of value is information about relevant learner abilities or traits.

Stage 4. Write Performance Objectives - Skills and attitudes identified in stage 2 are rewritten as statements of observable (measurable) behavior. They guide instruction by indicating the class of behavior intended and consequently the requisite conditions of learning. They also provide a blueprint for evaluation.

Stage 5. Develop Criterion-Referenced Test Items - The preparation of performance measures or tests immediately follows the writing of performance objectives in order to assure congruence between objectives and evaluation of learning outcomes. The term "criterion-referenced" accentuates this point by specifying a performance objective as the criterion for which each test item is to be referenced.

Stage 6. Developing Instructional Strategy - An instructional strategy is a plan for facilitating learners' achievement. Planning the instructional strategy, whether for teacher-centered or self-contained instruction, precedes development of materials. During this stage, attention is directed to providing the necessary events of instruction. The choice of delivery system and the matching of media to objectives and events of instruction constitute major categories of decisions made by the designer at this stage.

Stage 7. Develop or Select Instructional Materials - Instructional materials are media, whatever their form, that address events of instruction. In this stage, materials are developed and /or selected to most effectively deliver the desired events.

Stage 8. Design and Conduct Formative Evaluation - This stage involves the tryout and revision of instructional materials. It represents a feedback loop in which materials are tested with learners to obtain the necessary data for changes needed to improve initially developed materials. The goal of formative evaluation is to perfect the instruction so that it is optimal for the most students.

Stage 9. Design and Conduct Summative Evaluation - The last stage involves evaluation of an entire system of instruction. It is accomplished by studying the results of the instructional system after use by large numbers of students. This step provides data that are necessary for determining whether and how to implement a system on a wider scale.

i) (1) A procedural analysis reveals the steps or skills that are present in a procedure. It is essential for analyzing motor skills.

(2) In information processing analysis one seeks to describe the nature and sequence of the learners' thought processes that underlie the performance of any complex skill. One example would be describing the mental operations that one uses to balance a bank statement.

(3) Learning task analysis is designed to identify the enabling or prerequisite learnings contained in an intellectual skill. The results of learning task analysis facilitate proper sequencing of instruction.

j) The reasons for translating goal statements into performance objectives are that this :
    (1) enables one to communicate to different audiences who may require different levels of specificity
    (2) facilitates the development of instruction that is precisely matched to intended learning outcomes
    (3) guides the development of performance measures (criterion-referenced tests) that are highly correlated with previously stated performance objectives

k) The four (4) functions of performance objectives are to:
    (1) help judge the relationship between instruction and achievement of the goals
    (2) direct designers' attention to necessary conditions of learning
    (3) guide development of measures of learner performance that are congruent with learning outcomes
    (4) direct learners' attention so as to facilitate their learning (study) efforts

l) (1) According to Briggs, the three "anchor points" in planning are: (a)objectives, (b) instruction and (c)evaluation. It is essential that they be congruent with each other. This means that evaluation and instruction must be carefully related to objectives. The planning of objectives precedes the planning of evaluation and instruction.

    (2) The reasons for designing performance measures prior to instructional strategies are to:
        (a) help assure that the consistency between objectives and evaluation is maintained
        (b) avoid the tendency to unintentionally select measures that focus on content instead of more appropriate measures of performance

Criteria for Evaluating the Application Exercises:

1. The steps in the ID model are provided for in appropriate ways.

2. The steps in the model are logically ordered.

3. The relationship between successive steps is clear.

Example of an answer for the application exercise (yours could be completely different).

1. Study curriculm guides; consult with others in field of drama and apply personal expertise to make decisions regarding desired goals of program.

2. Consider characteristics of elementary school children of various ages. Think about their attitudes, cognitive and physical abilities, and any enabling skills that might be essential for accomplishing program goals. Adjust goals accordingly.

3. Apply instructional analysis to goals in order to identify which specific learnings are to be taught. (Which learning outcomes are derived from the program goals?)

4. Specify learnings from instructional analysis by writing performance objectives for the entire curriculum.

5. Prepare test items that match the learning outcomes specified in the performance objectives for the program.

6. Determine how to best present the course. Consider whether teacher-centered or mediated materials (and if so which type(s) would be most effective and for which learning outcomes. How might role playing and cooperative learning tasks be used to achieve desired instructional events?

7. Review materials to determine which ones can be used or adapted. Decide what materials or learning experiences need to be developed and develop them.

8. Try out all parts of the course of study for your drama program with small groups of students or with a few classes. Gather information to evaluate how well students responded and learned from your materials and/or presentations. Have students reflect on their experience with the "trial course."

9. Prepare to evaluate the drama curriculum after it has been operating for a year. Involve teachers and students in the evaluation and carefully analyze results before making any modifications to program.

NOTES

THE OUTCOMES OF INSTRUCTION

Overview:

This chapter examines the classification of different types of educational and instructional outcomes. These outcomes are classified according to specificity (goals vs. objectives) and types (information vs. skills). The reason for classifying learning outcomes into types of learning is based on the premise that different types of outcomes require different types of instructional treatments.

This chapter concentrates initially on verbal information, but the important capability to be developed is the recognition of examples of the five major categories of learning (Objective 2), i.e., classifying outcomes according to learning type. When you are presented with descriptions of instructional activities, assessment items, or subject matter content, you should be able to name the type of learning involved. First, study the terms and their relationships and then, practice classifying the types of learning. A further classification of intellectual skills is presented in Chapter 4.

Objectives:

1. **When asked, in the form of an oral or written question, state**

    a) the definitions of educational goal and objective. Include an example of each.

    b) the differences and similarities between goals and objectives.

    c) the relationships among educational goals, human capabilities, objectives, courses, and instruction.

    d) the five major categories of human capabilities.

    e) the major reasons for distinguishing among these five categories.

    f) the definitions of verbal information, motor skill, attitude, intellectual skill, and cognitive strategy, with examples of each category of learning.

2. **Given a list of assorted learning tasks, classify examples** of verbal information, motor skills, attitudes, intellectual skills, and cognitive strategies by labeling.

Practice Exercises:

1. a) Define educational goal and educational objective, give an example of each.

b) List the differences and similarities between a goal and an objective.

(differences)

(similarities)

c) (1) Describe the relationships among educational goals, human capabilities, objectives, courses, and instruction.

c) (2) Give examples of each of the following.

(a) Human Capability:

(b) Objective:

(c) Course

(d) Instruction

d) List the five major categories of learned capabilities. Next to each, write its definition with one example.

(1) _____ :

(2) _____ :

(3) _____ :

(4) _____ :

(5) _____ :

e) Briefly describe the major reasons why teachers or instructors or trainers should develop the ability to tell the differences among the types of learning.

f) On the line to the left of each definition in column A, write the letter from column B for the term being defined. Each term in column B may be used once, more than once, or not at all.

Column A

___1. Specific statements of learning outcomes.

___2. Recalling or summarizing memorized details.

___3. The arrangement of events that facilitate learning.

___4. A capability which makes symbol or concept use possible.

___5. A capability which allows a person to control muscular movements to accomplish an action.

___6. An internal process governing a person's learning and thinking behavior.

___7. Broad descriptions of human activities that are of societal importance.

___8. An internal affective state that influences personal choices.

___9. The acquired knowledge, skills, or attitudes essential for performing human activities.

___10. Learning how to do something of an intellectual nature.

___11. Declarative knowledge.

___12. A performance involving bodily movement.

Column B

a. Attitude

b. Cognitive Strategy

c. Conditions of Learning

d. Course

e. Educational Goals

f. Human Capabilities

g. Instruction

h. Intellectual Skill

i. Motor Skill

j. Objectives

k. Systems Approach

l. Verbal Information

2A.   Classify the following learning outcomes as (A) Attitude, (CS) Cognitive Strategy, (IS) Intellectual Skill, (MS) Motor Skill, or (VI) Verbal Information. Write the initials of the type of learning to the left of each task. Record the numbers of the items you answer incorrectly, then isolate your classification weaknesses using the matrix at the end of this chapter.

_____   1. A student uses a mnemonic device to learn the colors of the rainbow.

_____   2. From a list of descriptions of actions taken after a person's arrest for a crime, students indicate those items representing procedural due process.

_____   3. Underline the words in a paragraph that should have been capitalized.

_____   4. List the planks in the platform of each presidential candidate.

_____   5. Use a power saw to cut a sheet of plywood.

_____   6. Design an air-conditioning system for a warehouse.

_____   7. Bend copper tubing and weld it to a refrigerator condenser.

_____   8. A student regularly checks out science fiction novels from the library for leisure reading.

_____   9. A soldier assembles an M-16 rifle in 3 minutes.

_____   10. Summarize the major parts of the Constitution.

_____   11. Arrange the battles of the Civil War in chronological order.

_____   12. Operate a 16mm movie projector.

_____   13. When presented with a chemistry assignment, one student stops and thinks about the problem, researches related information, and develops a plan to solve the problem. Another student's approach is to use trial and error.

_____   14. Write a business letter in proper format.

_____   15. At every opportunity Alex attends country and western concerts.

_____   16. Students in political science learn to recognize newspaper editorials as conservative, liberal or moderate.

_____   17. Determine how many sheets of plywood are required to build a doghouse.

_____   18. Name the major farm products of several regions in the U.S.

_____   19. Bisect an angle using a compass.

_____   20. Bill remembers people to whom he has been introduced by associating a physical object with that person.

_____   21. Students are given a list of descriptions which are either budgets, accounts receivable, or accounts payable and are asked to match each description with its type.

_____ 22. Write the German equivalents to a list of English words.

_____ 23. Treat others courteously.

_____ 24. Write a computer program which generates mailing labels.

_____ 25. Match a list of dates with events in European history.

2B.   Classify the following learning outcomes as (A) Attitude, (CS) Cognitive Strategy, (IS) Intellectual Skill, (MS) Motor Skill, or (VI) Verbal Information. Write the initials of the type of learning to the left of each task.

_____ 1. Serve a tennis ball.

_____ 2. Pronounce a new word when shown the printed word on a flash-card.

_____ 3. Play chess during free time.

_____ 4. Develop a way to remember the seven steps in an industrial process.

_____ 5. Apply a triangular bandage to an accident victim.

_____ 6. Define the term "collective bargaining."

_____ 7. A biology major consistently chooses English Literature courses to meet university elective requirements.

_____ 8. Describe the process used in arriving at a solution to a case study.

_____ 9. Plot the path of a hurricane using longitude and latitude.

_____ 10. Always buckle your seat belt in the driveway.

_____ 11. State Ohm's law.

_____ 12. Create an original recipe for a cake.

_____ 13. Perform correct blocking and tackling techniques in a football game.

_____ 14. Outline the approach followed in devising a new method for controlling air pollution.

_____ 15. Design a unique system for individualizing instruction.

_____ 16. Arrive at work on time every day.

_____ 17. State the tax law regarding earned income credit.

_____ 18. Compute the square root of a number.

_____ 19. Choose to use instructional programs rather than textbooks for teaching certain topics.

_____ 20. A tight-rope artist executes a flawless routine.

_____ 21. Draw instead of watch television.

_____ 22. Recite the alphabet from A to Z.

_____ 23. A basketball player shares with her coach how she went about developing a new offensive play.

_____ 24. Parallel park a car.

_____ 25. Develop an unusual approach for solving a problem -- an approach the instructor had never considered.

Application Exercises:

1. Obtain a curriculum guide or scope and sequence chart for a course with which you are familiar. Review the objectives for one or two units and classify them according to the five major categories of learning. Obtain feedback from your classmates and your instructor.

2. Locate a textbook for a course with which you are familiar. Review one or two chapters and classify the content according to the five major categories of learning. Obtain feedback from your classmates and your instructor.

Feedback for Practice Exercises:

1. a) An educational goal is a broad description of a human activity of significance to the functioning of society. It is a very general statement of learner outcomes which may be acquired: e.g., understanding mathematical operations; or, appreciating literature; or, applying scientific knowledge; or, knowing the principles of computer usage; or, developing a sense of citizenship.

   An objective is an unambiguous statement of a specific learning outcome:
   e.g., add two three-digit numbers with regrouping in 10s; or, recognize a metaphor; or, identify the nucleus of a cell; or, write a computer program for mailing labels; or, state the functions of the executive branch.

   b) Differences--
   A goal is broad, requires a long time frame, and is not easily measured.
   An objective is very precise, usually attainable in a short time frame, and is easily measured.
   Similarities--
   Both indicate learner outcomes or human capabilities and are content-related.

   c) Goals provide a general overview of a course. Objectives which specify precise human capabilities are derived from and support the goal. Instruction is the vehicle for developing the capabilities in students, thus achieving the objectives and goals for the course.

d) Verbal Information....   Declarative knowledge; recalling memorized facts, names, labels.

    e.g., stating the elements of the Fourth Amendment or recalling a phone number.

    Motor Skills..........   Coordinated muscular movements to achieve a particular purpose.

    e.g., using a can opener, jumping rope, drawing a straight line

    Attitudes.............   Internal states that affect choice decisions.

    e.g., listening to music in spare time, running regularly for exercise

    Intellectual Skills....   Capabilities making symbol or conceptualization use possible. They include learning how to perform an intellectual task involving concepts, rules, and problem- solving skills.

    e.g., identifying a rectangle, punctuating a sentence, making a weather prediction

    Cognitive Strategies..   Capabilities that govern one's learning and thinking behavior; internal control processes; learning strategies.

    e.g., using an image link to remember facts, using the inductive approach

e) Learning to differentiate among types of learning allows for:
1. the use of techniques appropriate for different types of learning outcomes
2. grouping of similar objectives
3. assessing the adequacy of coverage in each category in a course
4. the correct application of the conditions of learning
5. clarifying the specific human capabilities listed in curricular content

f) Matching Exercise:

1.	j	7.	e
2.	l	8.	a
3.	g	9.	f
4.	h	10.	h
5.	i	11.	l
6.	b	12.	i

2. Classification Exercise 2A

1.   CS Emphasis is on the mnemonic device as an internal process for managing the learning.
2.   IS Involves conceptualization.
3.   IS Uses symbols and concepts in doing something of an intellectual nature.
4.   VI Requires recall of memorized details.
5.   MS Involves primarily muscular coordination. (Note: Remembering the procedural steps to follow is actually VI.)
6.   IS This is a problem-solving task using concept and rule relationships.
7.   MS This physical task involves muscle coordination.
8.   A Reflects a choice of personal preference.
9.   MS Picking up and putting together is motor coordination. (Note: Recognizing the rifle parts would be IS.)

10. VI   Only possible if the elements were memorized at first.
11. VI   Sounds more complex but simply involves learning the correct order first.
12. MS   Physically manipulating the various controls...motor coordination.
13. CS   These students are using different strategies to accomplish the learning. The emphasis is on the internal process in use.
14. IS   Although writing is a motor skill, the significant learning there is the rule for formatting the letter correctly.
15. A   Indicates action based on personal preference or choice.
16. IS   Involves conceptualization...an intellectual endeavor.
17. IS   The student is solving a problem.
18. VI   The products have been recalled from memory.
19. MS   Requires physical manipulation of the compass.
20. CS   This describes Bill's strategy for remembering names and faces.
21. IS   Students are required to recognize concepts. Conceptualization is an intellectual activity.
22. VI   The vocabulary is committed to memory.
23. A   Courtesy requires choosing certain behaviors based on an internal affective state.
24. IS   To perform this task, one needs to apply intellectual relationships among symbols and concepts.
25. VI   The dates and events are memorized.

Classification Exercise 2B

1. MS   Uses control and coordination of muscular movements.
2. IS   Pronunciation is possible only if one applies language symbols and sounds (e.g., rules such as CVC/CVCe).
3. A   If one freely selects an activity in leisure time, such a choice reflects an attitude toward that activity.
4. CS   Although recalling the seven steps is VI, developing a way to remember is an internal learning strategy.
5. MS   Putting a bandage on is a physical skill requiring motor coordination.
6. VI   Only possible if the student has committed the definition to memory. Defining requires recall.
7. A   The literature classes are not compulsory. The free choice reflects personal preference.
8. CS   Whereas the solution to the case study is a product, the way they solved the problem outlines the internal process or strategy.
9. IS   The student is required to manipulate symbols and concepts to perform this task. Drawing the line is a motor skill but coordinate plotting is the prime learning, not the quality of line drawing.
10. A   This is an action which reflects internal feelings about safety.
11. VI   Depends upon memorization of the law.
12. IS   Involves the intellectual combination of symbols and concepts to solve the problem.
13. MS   A physical ability requiring muscle coordination.
14. CS   Emphasis is on the internal strategy for devising a solution.
15. IS   The creation of this instructional technique is a result of problem solving. (Note: Description of the approach used to develop this technique would be CS.)
16. A   Reflects the employee's personal choice.
17. VI   Requires factual recall from memory.
18. IS   Uses symbols in a procedural relationship.
19. A   The choice of technique is based on the internal affect of the instructor.

20. MS Precise, balanced motor coordination.
21. A Shows a positive inclination toward drawing.
22. VI The student has memorized the alphabet.
23. CS The player is outlining her strategy for creating the play.
24. MS Complex motor coordination.
25. CS The concern is with the approach (method, strategy, process) rather than with the product or solution.

Matrix for analyzing performance problems in practice exercises 2A and 2B

exercise A

Attitudes	8	15	23				
Cognitive Strategies	1	13	20				
Intellectual Skills	2	3	6	14	16	17	21	24
Motor Skills	5	7	9	12	19		
Verbal Information	4	10	11	18	22	25	

exercise B

Attitudes	3	7	10	16	19	21
Cognitive Strategies	4	8	14	23	25	
Intellectual Skills	2	9	12	15	18	
Motor Skills	1	5	13	20	24	
Verbal Information	6	11	17	22		

Here's a way to isolate your classification errors:

• Mark an "X" over the numbers of the items above that you answered incorrectly in the classification exercise.

• The numbers in any particular row correspond to the type of learning listed at left.

• If you had more than one error in any row, reread the part of the text that deals with the type of learning that you are not classifying correctly.

What kind of error have you made?

• The domains and sub-domains you have been learning are themselves defined concepts.

• Some research (e.g., Tennyson, Wooley, & Merrill, 1972) suggests that there are three types of concept error:

Overgeneralizing is classifying a nonexample as an instance of the class of concepts.

Undergeneralization is rejecting an example by having too narrow a view of the concept.

Misconception occurs when you use the wrong attributes to classify an example of the concept.

• When you reread the text, try to figure out what type of error you made.

Criteria for Evaluating the Application Exercises:

1. Is the student performance implied in the content consistent with the assigned category of learning?

2. Is the content classified into multiple categories when appropriate?
    (e.g., verbal information <u>and</u> intellectual skills for the content "metaphor" which suggests both a definition and a concept)

3. Is <u>all</u> content accounted for in the categories of learning?

Examples of Application Exercise:

EXAMPLE 1. Classification of the goals for French I (grades 9-11) as listed in a curriculum guide.

<u>Intellectual Skills</u>

The students will learn to:
1. understand instructions given in French
2. comprehend simple readings outside of the textbook
3. self-express orally on an elementary level, using proper pronunciation, grammar, and vocabulary.
4. self-express in written form on an elementary level, using proper grammar and vacabulary
5. use cognates (French/English) to aid comprehension of readings in French
6. discriminate auditorily and apply French phonetic sounds
7. generate dialogues based on grammar and vocabulary taught
8. conjugate regular and irregular verbs
9. apply verb reflexivity
10. use *passé composé* and *imparfait*
11. use the future and conditional tenses

<u>Verbal Information</u>

The students will learn:
1. the vocabulary and appropriate gender within the context of each unit
2. the verbs requiring reflexive pronouns
3. the basic geography of France
4. the French culture and mentality

<u>Motor Skills</u>

1. The students will learn to articulate the French "r" and vowels (nasals).

<u>Cognitive Strategies</u>

1. The students will develop methods to facilitate vocabulary acquisition.

<u>Attitudes</u>

The students will choose to believe:
1. that bilingualism is less a luxury capability than it was formerly thought to be
2. that second language acquisition can be enjoyable and can open many doors that might otherwise be closed to them

EXAMPLE 2. Classification of the learnings in a unit on weather in a kindergarten science course.

<u>Intellectual Skills</u>

1. Recognize sources of heat.
   Heat sources are objects that produce heat and are hot to touch.
2. Recognize helpful and harmful weather.
   Helpful weather enables us to accomplish a particular task more easily. Harmful weather may cause us fear or injury and causes us to take precautions against it.
3. Provide a solution for keeping a snowman at a warm period of the year.
4. Given pictures of the different seasons, identify what season it is by responding orally.
5. Identify pictures of cumulus, nimbus, stratus, and cirrus clouds.

<u>Verbal Information</u>

1. Provided with a tree representing each season, list the activities performed during that season by cutting and pasting the activities beside the appropriate tree.
2. List the four seasons in sequential order.
3. Give the definitions of helpful weather, harmful weather, and heat sources.

<u>Attitudes</u>

1. Choose to express interest in the weather as reflected in comments about the daily weather conditions.

<u>Motor Skills</u>

1. Upon hearing the tornado warning alarm, assume the correct position by crouching down on your knees with your head down to the floor and arms and hands covering your head.

INTELLECTUAL SKILLS AND COGNITIVE STRATEGIES

Overview:

Chapter 4 considers two very important types of learning: intellectual skills and problem solving. Intellectual skills are broken into several subcategories: discriminations, concrete concepts, defined concepts, rules, and problem solving (often associated with problem solving). Cognitive strategies, which is a special type of intellectual skill, have no subcategories although future research may suggest that cognitive strategies should be subdivided.

As you proceed through this chapter focus on the performances which are exhibited through different learned capabilities. Also, pay attention to the distinctive internal and external conditions required by the different types of learning. Examples are provided to help in classifying types of intellectual skills and cognitive strategies. Keep track of the types of errors you are making and use the matrix at the end of the learner's guide chapter to isolate these.

Finally, learn the vocabulary. Technical terminology is a necessary part of the instructional designer's toolbox.

Objectives:

1. **When asked, in the form of an oral or written question, state:**

    a) in your own words why intellectual skills are such important learned capabilities

    b) five types of intellectual skills by levels of complexity

    c) why it is important to consider intellectual skills in terms of their levels of complexity

    d) a definition of "cognitive strategies"

    e) how cognitive strategies differ from other intellectual skills

    f) three different strategies a learner might apply to improve learning

    g) a definition of "metacognition," and explain how it may be demonstrated by the learner

    h) three different positions regarding the teaching and learning of general problem-solving strategies

    i) the difference between the way an expert and a novice approaches problem-solving situations

2. **Given a list of performances of intellectual skills and cognitive strategies, classify** them according to the learning type they represent by matching the characteristic to the learning type.

3. **Given a list of the internal conditions for learning intellectual skills and cognitive strategies, classify** them according to the learning type they represent by matching the internal conditions to the learning type.

4. **Given a list of external conditions for learning intellectual skills and cognitive strategies, classify** them according to the learning types they represent by matching the external condition to the learning type.

5. **Given a list of learning outcomes in the intellectual skills and cognitive strategy domains, classify** them according to the type of learning they represent.

Practice Exercises:

1. a) Why are intellectual skills such important learned capabilities? Briefly describe (one or two sentences).

    b) List five types of intellectual skills in order of their complexity from the simplest to the most complex.

    _____ (simplest)

    _____

    _____

    _____

    _____ (most complex)

    c) Why is the level of complexity important to consider when learning intellectual skills? Explain.

    d) Write a two-word definition of "cognitive strategy."   _____ _____.

    e) How do cognitive strategies differ from other intellectual skills? Describe.

f) Briefly describe how a learner uses the following types of strategies according to Weinstein and Mayer:
(1) rehearsal strategies

(2) elaboration strategies

(3) organizing strategies

(4) comprehension monitoring strategies

(5) affective strategies

g) Define the term "metacognition," and briefly explain how learners can demonstrate metacognitive knowledge.

h) Briefly describe three different positions regarding the "teachability" of problem-solving skills?

(1)

(2)

(3)

i) Studies, contrasting experts and novices, have found that experts do not necessarily have better problem-solving strategies than novices. What makes experts more efficient at problem-solving? Explain what is implied by this research?

2. Classify each of the performances below by writing one of the following intellectual skills or cognitive strategy capabilities in the space provided: (D) discriminations; (CC) concrete concepts; (DC) defined concepts; (R) rules; (PS) problem solving; (CS) cognitive strategies.

_____ a) Observing a physical object, Harry identifies instances of a class of object properties including positions of the objects.

_____ b) As a part of her job, Sharon must distinguish stimuli that differ on one or more physical dimensions.

_____ c) As a philosopher, Marie must follow a definition in classifying an object or relationship.

_____ d) As a teacher, David must often synthesize rules to create novel solutions.

_____ e) As part of her speech assignment, Jan was asked to explain in writing how she prepared for the speech.

_____ f) To prove that he has learned to use the Pythagorean theorem, Rick demonstrates its application.

3. Classify each of the conditions within the learner (internal conditions) below by writing one of the following intellectual skills or cognitive strategy capabilities in the space provided: (D) discriminations; (CC) concrete concepts; (DC) defined concepts; (R) rules; (PS) problem solving (CS) cognitive strategies.

_____ a) In playing complicated war games, Otto retrieves relevant information and subordinate rules.

_____ b) In pointing out the various types of trucks on the highway, Peggy retrieves discriminations.

_____ c) Using his study method in preparing for a final exam, John retrieves concepts, simple rules, and required verbal directions.

_____ d) While wine tasting, Jean detects subtle differences in the aroma among wines.

_____ e) In applying her lifesaving skills, Cindy retrieves relevant concepts.

_____ f) In learning to use psychological constructs, Haley retrieves relevant component concepts included in the definition.

4. Classify each of the conditions in the learning situation (external conditions) below by writing one of the following intellectual skills or cognitive strategy capabilities in the space provided: (D) discriminations; (CC) concrete concepts; (DC) defined concepts; (R) rules; (PS) problem solving; (CS) cognitive strategies.

_____ a) verbal definition and a number of different examples and nonexamples.

_____ b) often minimum verbal cues, but learner must be aware of the goal of the activity.

_____ c) results from discovery or, alternately, verbal instructions or demonstrations.

_____ d) permits a selection and provides selective reinforcement.

_____ e) verbal communications remind learner of component. concepts; guide learner to arrange them in proper order

_____ f) physical instances which vary widely in nonrelevant characteristics are presented.

5A.

Directions. The situations below represent various kinds of intellectual skills or cognitive strategies. Classify each example by writing one of the following choices in the blank following the example: (D) discrimination; (CC) concrete concept; (DC) defined concept; (R) rule; (PS) problem solving; (CS) cognitive strategy. The correct answers are provided at the end of the exercise.

• Mark the numbers of the items you answer incorrectly, then isolate your classification weaknesses using the matrix at the end of this chapter.

1. In a high school economics course, students learn the law of supply and demand. That is, they learn to predict what will happen to prices if supplies are increased and demand is decreased. When students have learned the law of supply and demand and can predict whether prices will rise or fall, they have learned a _____.

2. When students in a high school English course can label types of poetry (e.g., sonnet, ballad, etc.) for poems that they have not seen before, they are showing that they have learned a _____.

3. The boy on a TV ad can tell when his mother has washed his sweater in a different soap because it feels different. He is showing _____ learning.

4. During basic training in the Army, the soldier learns to identify four kinds of tanks. This ability is called _____ learning.

5. In a test in a science class, the teacher lays various strands of cotton and silk fiber on the table and has students name each strand as being either cotton or silk. This test is measuring _____ learning.

6. If a course on world cultures requires students to develop solutions to India's depressed economic situation, students are demonstrating _____ learning.

7. In chemistry class students are given various problem situations to solve throughout the course. One student, in solving the problems, stops and thinks about the problem, looks up related information on the problem, and develops a plan for solving the problem. Another student's approach is to solve the problems by trial and error experiments. These two students are exhibiting different _____.

8. In a physical education class, students must learn the difference between a bump and a spike. When they see a player doing one action (a bump) they name it as a bump. When they see a player doing another type of action, they name it a spike. Learning to name actions bumps or spikes is called _____ learning.

9. When spear fishing, Charles knows he must aim the spear below the fish because of the way light bends when it passes through water. Charles is showing that he has learned a _____.

10. A corporation rewards one of its employees for developing an original system for recycling used papers by providing a one-week expense-paid vacation in Florida. The company is rewarding the use of _____ by its employees.

11. In a business management course, students must learn types of economic organizations (e.g., subsistence economics, planned economics, or market economics). When students have learned to determine the economic organization of a country, they have learned _____.

12. A major corporation provides a series of workshops in creative management for its top-level managers. These workshops present a variety of novel problems to assist the employer in discovering innovative ways of solving complex problems. These workshops are designed to foster _____.

5B.

1. In a social studies class, students learn about different types of propaganda. When they have learned the types of propaganda such as name calling, glittering generalities, and bandwagon, they will have learned _____.

2. In a science unit dealing with taxonomies, students are presented with various types of plants and rocks. Students are then told to make up their own system for grouping the items (i.e., they are told to develop new classification systems). This task represents _____.

3. By the end of the course on refrigeration and air conditioning, students should be able to design an air-conditioning system for a given building. Students must design a system with appropriate types of controls, compressors, electric motors, electric circuits, and refrigerants. Demonstration of this skill represents _____ learning.

4. Referring to a picture on a worksheet, the teacher says, "See the figure next to the happy face? Draw a line from it to the one that is just like it on the the other side." This task is measuring _____ learning.

5. In an art class the teacher hands Marion a sheet of rough sandpaper and tells her, "Close your eyes and pick up a sheet of sandpaper from the pile on the table in front of you. Tell me which sheets are the same as the one in your hand now." When Marion can do this, she is demonstrating _____ learning.

6. In a social studies class, students learn to interpret data from a graphical form (e.g., bar graph showing the number of soldiers killed in Civil War battles). When students can interpret data presented in graphical form, they have learned _____.

7. In a drafting course, students are required to demonstrate orthographic projections by drawing orthographic views of an object which is presented in one-dimensional view. Assuming that students have the motor skills of drawing lines and that direct instruction is provided for the task, the skill of drawing orthographic views represents _____ learning.

8. When the music instructor requires his students to reproduce a note which sounds the same as the note he produced, the instructor is requiring students to demonstrate _____ learning in addition to motor learning.

9. In preparing for a big exam, John likes to review his notes a week before the exam and again two days before. The night before an exam, he usually takes in a movie. Dan, however, studies only the night before and uses old exams, which he memorizes. These two students are employing different _____.

10. In an air-conditioning and refrigeration course, one unit deals with parts of a refrigerator. One objective of the unit is that students know the parts. The test includes the presentation of three or four refrigerators of different makes. Students would be required to point to each part when the instructor states the name. This task represents _____ learning.

11. Some students are better at interpreting political cartoons than others are. When asked to explain how they interpret cartoons, most will describe their personal approach to this task. Their explanation describes _____ category of learning.

12. Trainees in a Navy basic electronics class are asked to point out the components of a schematic. Sailors who can perform this task are exhibiting _____ learning.

Application Exercise:

1. Using the application exercise from Chapter 3, classify the objectives you labeled as intellectual skills into their learning types (discrimination, concrete concepts, defined concepts, rules, and problem solving).

2. Take a content area with which you are familiar and try to identify one problem-solving skill associated with that content, two rules associated with that problem-solving skill, and two concepts associated with one of the rules. Write them in the form of learning outcomes.

Feedback for Practice Exercises:

1. a) Intellectual skills make it possible for individuals to use symbols to respond to their environment through the use of symbols.

    b) From simplest to most complex: discrimination, concrete concepts, defined concepts, rules, and problem solving.

    c) It is a characteristic of intellectual skills that the learning of complex skills depends on the prior learning of simpler skills.

    d) Cognitive strategies have the learner's own cognitive processes as their objects, whereas intellectual skills are oriented toward environmental objects and events.

    e) A cognitive strategy is a control process by which a learner selects and modifies attention, learning, remembering, and thinking.

    f) Any three of the strategies listed below:

       (1) The learner conducts her own practice of the material being learned (i.e., rehearsal).

       (2) The learner deliberately associates the learning material with other readily accessible material (e.g., paraphrasing, note taking).

       (3) The learner arranges the material to be learned into an organized framework of meaningful categories.

       (4) The learner sets goals, estimates the success with which the goals are being met, and selects alternative strategies to meet the goals.

       (5) The learner uses these strategies to control anxiety, maintain attention, or manage learning time.

    g) Metacognition is the internal processing that uses cognitive strategies to control and monitor other learning and memory processes.

       When learners are aware of their metacognitive strategies and describe them, they are demonstrating metacognitive knowledge.

h) (1) General problem-solving strategies can be taught and will generalize to other situations.

(2) General problem-solving strategies can be taught, but are most likely to develop indirectly from task-specific strategies.

(3) General problem-solving strategies are teachable, but not very useful for specific problem-solving tasks.

i) Experts approach problem solving with better organized knowledge bases, a great deal of subject-specific verbal information and intellectual skills. According to Gagné and Glaser (1987), "... when experts look at an apparently complicated situation, they are able to represent it in terms of a small number of chunks" (page 69).

2. a) concrete concepts
   b) discriminations
   c) defined concepts
   d) problem solving
   e) cognitive strategies
   f) rules

3. a) problem solving
   b) concrete concepts
   c) cognitive strategies
   d) discriminations
   e) rules
   f) defined concepts

4. a) defined concepts
   b) problem solving
   c) cognitive strategies
   d) discriminations
   e) rules
   f) concrete concepts

5. Feedback for Exercises 5A & 5B

EXERCISE A	EXERCISE B
1) rule	1) defined concept
2) defined concept	2) problem solving
3) discrimination	3) problem solving
4) concrete concept	4) discrimination
5) concrete concept	5) discrimination
6) problem solving	6) rule
7) cognitive strategy	7) rule
8) defined concept	8) discrimination
9) rule	9) cognitive strategy
10) problem solving	10) concrete concept
11) defined concept	11) cognitive strategy
12) cognitive strategy	12) concrete concept

Classification feedback matrix for practice exercises 5A & 5B

	exercise 5A				exercise 5B		
Discriminations	3				4	5	8
Concrete Concepts	4	5			10	12	
Defined Concepts	2	8	11		1		
Rules	1	9			6	7	
Problem Solving	6	10			2	3	
Cognitive Strategies	7	12			9	11	

<u>Here's a way to isolate your classification errors:</u>

• Mark an "X" over the numbers of the items that you answered incorrectly in the classification exercise.

• The numbers in any particular row correspond to the type of learning listed at left.

• If you had more than one error in any row, reread the part of the text that deals with the type of learning that you are not classifying correctly.

<u>What kind of error have you made?</u>

• The domains and sub-domains you have been learning are themselves defined concepts.

• Some research (e.g., Tennyson, Wooley, & Merrill, 1972) suggests that there are three types of concept error:

<u>Overgeneralizing</u> is classifying a nonexample as an instance of the class of concepts.

<u>Undergeneralization</u> is rejecting an example by having too narrow a view of the concept.

<u>Misconception</u> occurs when you use the wrong attributes to classify an example of the concept.

• When you reread the text, try to figure out what type of error you made.

Criteria for Evaluating the Application Exercise:

1. Classification criteria - The objectives are broken down into their component rules, concepts and discriminations.

2. Problem-solving skill - The problem-solving skill subsumes at least two rules.

   The rule-using skill subsumes at least two concepts.

Examples of the Application Exercise:

1. (Classifying intellectual skills from learner's guide Chapter 3 into sub-domains)
   a) understand instructions given in French [discriminations, defined concepts, and rules]
   b) comprehend simple readings of the textbook [discriminations, concrete concepts, defined concepts, and rules]
   c) self-express orally on an elementary level, using proper grammar and vocabulary [discriminations, defined concepts, and rules]
   d) self-express in written form on an elementary level, using proper grammar and vocabulary [discriminations, defined concepts, and rules]
   e) use cognates (French/English) to aid comprehension of readings in French [rules]
   f) discriminate auditorily and apply French phonetic sounds [discriminations, concrete concepts, defined concepts, and rules]
   g) generate dialogues based on grammar and vocabulary taught [rules, problem-solving]
   h) conjugate regular and irregular verbs [rules]
   i) apply verb reflexivity [rules]
   j) use *passé composé* and *imparfait* [defined concepts, rules]
   k) use the future and conditional tenses [rules]

2. All content areas use problem-solving skills, rules, and concepts. So, you have much to choose from. Consider the area of music. To compose a symphony, a problem-solving task, you need to know many rules. For example, you need to know the rules for writing music notation. These include more specific rules such as the one concerning writing the name of a major key when given a staff with a key signature. Of course, you cannot learn this rule until you have first mastered the concepts: major key, staff, and key signature. Does your example also show a relationship among problem solving, rules, and concepts?

   The student will compose a symphony. (problem solving)

   The student will write music notation for 10 instruments playing simultaneously. (rule)

   The student will write notation in a specified key siganture. (rule)

   The student will classify major and minor key signatures. (concept)

   The student will classify types of musical staffs. (concept)

NOTES

INFORMATION, ATTITUDES, AND MOTOR SKILLS

Overview:

Chapter 5 continues the discussion of Gagné's taxonomy of learning outcomes by discussing the domains of verbal information, attitudes and motor skills. The learning outcomes for this chapter parallel those from Chapter 4. While reading the chapter, focus on: a) the performance characteristics of each of the three domains, b) the internal conditions that must be present for these categories of learning to occur and c) the external conditions needed to facilitate the acquisition of each domain. Secondly, it is crucial that you learn these three domains so that you can accurately classify instances of each whenever they are encountered. Learning activities include writing requisite information and practice in classifying examples of verbal information, attitudes and motor skills.

Study activities for this chapter include: 1) tasks requiring recall of information about the conditions of learning and the performance characteristics of each domain of learning, and 2) practice in classifying examples of each domain. Use the feedback matrices to detect error patterns, which will indicate areas of needed practice. The application exercises for this chapter will build on those skills from chapters 3, and 4, and challenge you to apply the taxonomy in the analysis of instructional materials.

Objectives:

1. When presented with an oral or written question, state:
    a) definitions for the three varieties of verbal information learning
    b) definition of attitude learning
    c) definition of motor skill learning

    d) the major reason for learning some verbal information to a high degree of certainty

    e) two reasons for acquiring general knowledge

    f) the characteristics of performance for (1) facts, (2) organized knowledge, (3) attitudes, and (4) motor skills, by writing a one or two sentence description of each

    g) in your own words, the internal and external conditions for (1) facts, (2) organized knowledge, (3) attitudes, and (4) motor skills.

2. **Given a list of learner performances, classify** them as verbal information, attitudes or motor skills.

3. **Given instructional materials, classify** the possible outcomes from those materials by making a list of content organized by types of learning.

Practice Exercises:

1. Define and give one example of:
   a) the three varieties of verbal information known as labels, facts and organized knowledge.

   b) attitude learning

   c) motor skill learning.

   d) What is the major reason for learning some types of information to a high degree of certainty?

   e) Give two reasons for having students acquire general knowledge through formal education.
   (1)

   (2)

   f) (1) What performance indicates that a fact or organized knowledge has been learned?

   (2) How does a learner show that an attitude has been learned?

   (3) How does a learner show that a motor skill has been learned?

g) (1) What are the internal conditions of learning for facts and organized knowledge?

(2) What are the internal conditions of learning for attitudes?

(3) What are the internal conditions of learning for motor skills?

2A. Classify the following 15 descriptions of human behavior and performance into one of the following learning categories: Verbal Information (VI), Attitude (A), Motor Skills (MS).

___1. Linda stays after school almost every Friday to help her science teacher prepare the weekly lab exercise.

___2. Len can name all of the U.S. Army generals who served during World War II.

___3. Arnold is extremely accurate at putting a golf ball.

___4. A student goes to the library to read *Sports Illustrated*.

___5. The learner can list the African countries that border on the Sahara.

___6. Mr. Stevens takes in the annual Newport Jazz Festival each summer.

___7. Tracy can catch a softball.

___8. Cary likes to play with Jane rather than Susan.

___9. My students can recite the Gettysburg Address.

___10. Although only 10 years of age, Nadia already showed extraordinary ability on the balance beam.

___11. The students were asked to write a definition for antonym and synonym.

___12. Elementary students almost always enjoy PE.

___13. I will ask my students to describe the process of photosynthesis.

___14. You have to be able to eat with chopsticks at some Chinese restaurants.

___15. Seventh-grade students can describe how penicillin was discovered.

2B. For additional practice, classify this second set of statements of human behavior and performance using the same three domains of learning as in exercise 2a.

__1.   Mr. Lofton's teams have always been noted for their fine sportsmanship.

__2.   If a child can trace a number, he is well on his way to writing it.

__3.   Students are asked to name the major farm products of the Southeast region of the U.S.

__4.   Students learn to use a power hand saw to cut a sheet of plywood following a straight line.

__5.   Students should be able to write the rule for computing the hypotenuse of a triangle.

__6.   Most instructors would rather focus their attention on teaching than on evaluation.

__7.   When students are asked to explain the reasons for the decline of the Roman Empire, they can give the five major reasons.

__8.   Anna reads lots of romance novels.

__9.   My grandfather still thinks the best car you can buy is a Chevy.

__10. Robin can replace the oil filter on a car.

__11. Students can list the top priorities of the Democratic presidential platform of 1988.

__12. Scouts learn to make a fire by rubbing sticks together.

__13. Johnny told his parents the procedure for getting excused from class.

__14. Jason knows how to shave with a razor.

__15. My daughter is always eager to go to the beach.

2C. The following summary task for chapters 3-5 will help you assess your skill in classifying all categories of learnings in Gagné's taxonomy. Using the nine types of learning from Gagné's taxonomy, classify each description of learner behavior by writing the abbreviation of the type of learning in the space provided. The abbreviations are: Cognitive Strategy (CS); Motor Skill (MS); Attitude (A); Verbal Information (VI); Discrimination (D); Concrete Concept (CC); Defined Concept (DC); Rule (R); Higher-order Rule (HR).

__   1.   Students are presented with an Elizabethan poem and are asked to mark each instance of alliteration contained in the poem. Such a response represents which type of learning?

__   2.   Students are given papers containing pictures of squares and are asked to trace the squares. When students exhibit this performance, they reveal what learned capability?

___ 3. A student uses a set of date associations to learn the names of people who participated in several historical events. This behavior constitutes an example of what type of learning?

___ 4. Students are planning to build a doghouse and are asked to determine how many sheets of plywood are required to build the house. Completing this task indicates what type of learning?

___ 5. Students are asked to spell a new word that contains an 'ie' sequence (such as believe). When students can successfully spell new words with the 'ie' sequence, what learning do they show?

___ 6. A student goes to the library and reads during most free periods at school. Such behavior is best characterized as revealing what type of learning?

___ 7. Students in drivers education are asked to park a car in a space that is parallel to the curb. Parallel parking is an example of what type of learning?

___ 8. When given a set of 10 pairs of X-rays of the hip bone, a student in medical school marks an 'x' on each pair that has a consistent appearance in bone density. When students can accurately match all pairs that share similar patterns of bone density, they have exhibited which type of learning?

___ 9. Students in an introductory art class learn to differentiate among various art media. When the response called for involves writing the name of the medium (e.g., oil, pastel, etc.) used in each of 20 paintings, what type of learning is indicated?

___ 10. Students can match the authors of the current top10 list for fiction with the titles of the books. This constitutes an example of which type of learning?

___ 11. A student states for his teacher how he visualizes a map so that he can recall the location of all the Canadian provinces. This self-described behavior is an example of which learning?

___ 12. Students who are given sentences in declarative form and must then restate the sentences in interrogative form are exhibiting what type of learning?

___ 13. What learning is measured when a pupil is asked to pick out all the rectangles in the classroom?

___ 14. Students have been asked to prepare for a test in social studies using their textbook and notes from class. On this test they will be asked to write in their own words the reasons most frequently given for the U.S. Civil War. Such a performance represents what type of learning?

___ 15. In a drafting class students must learn to draw lines of a certain thickness and precision using the T-square. What type of learning makes such a performance possible?

___ 16. At the conclusion of a course in media production, a final project might involve the student being given a unit of instruction for which mediated instruction is to be developed. Such an assignment would represent which learning?

___ 17. A geometry student is able to differentiate between ellipses and circles based on information which is given about the distance from the center of all other points. In so doing, the student demonstrates what type of learning?

___ 18. In a class on diagnosis for learning disabilities, students typically go about their search for an accurate diagnosis in different ways. These different ways may be thought of as which type of learning?

___ 19. When students can write the names of each of the states in the USSR, they have demonstrated what type of learning?

___ 20. The student who elects to join the French club rather than the history club is demonstrating which type of learning?

___ 21. In a biology class the teacher gives the students a mounted slide (X) and asks them to find the slide from a set of six additional mounted slides that looks the same as slide (X). When the student successfully performs this task he demonstrates which type of learning?

___ 22. In a photography class students are given instruction in determining proper settings for different lighting conditions. When students use this knowledge to make camera setting adjustments in accordance with various lighting conditions, they are demonstrating which type of learning?

___ 23. A student is given sample leaves from the various species of maple trees that are native to Canada. The student is required to name each of the 12 leaves that the teacher presents. The student is demonstrating what type of learning?

___ 24. In an English class students are learning library research skills. Prior to the conclusion of the unit, the teacher gives an ungraded library assignment that requires the use of a variety of skills, including one that the teacher did not yet teach. Completion of this assignment illustrates which type of learning?

___ 25. An instructor wishes to assess his students' ability to differentiate between monopolies and cartels. Verbal descriptions of various businesses are given and students respond by designating each description as either a monopoly or a cartel or neither. Through this performance, students are demonstrating what type of learning?

___ 26. In a kindergarten class teachers are giving students a lesson on the sense of taste. When children can show that they can tell sour tastes from sweet tastes by making a distinctly sour expression to food substances that are sour, they exhibit what type of learning?

___ 27. More and more teachers have decided to avoid the use of corporal punishment as a technique for managing students' behavior. Avoidance of corporal punishment is indicative of which type of learning?

Application Exercises:

1. Select a textbook chapter (any subject), an instructional manual, a curriculum guide for a particular grade level, or any instructional software. Identify two or three examples of each of the types of learning from Gagné's taxonomy, if possible. Of course, depending on the subject chosen, there will be some categories of learning that will be much easier to locate than others. Some may be missing altogether. Be alert to those cases where multiple learning outcomes are to be achieved from the same content or topic, especially information and concepts, rules, and higher-order rules.

2. A second enlightening and instructive task is to analyze one of your old tests, again from any course, to determine exactly what types of learning were measured. How might certain measures (individual test items or sections of the test) have been modified to assess a different class of learning based on the same content? Consult your instructor if you are uncertain of any of the examples of learning that you examine in your analysis.

Feedback for Practice Exercises:

1. a) <u>Label</u> - the name given to an object or object class (e.g., banana, fruit).

    <u>Fact</u> - a statement that expresses a relation between two or more named objects or events (e.g., Columbus discovered America in 1492).

    <u>Organized knowledge</u> - verbal information in the form of networks of interconnected propositions or facts (e.g., the causes of the American Civil War or the antecedents of US military involvement in Vietnam).

    b) Attitude - a psychological state that predisposes one to act in specific ways toward people, things, events or ideas. Comprised of cognitive and affective components. May have narrow focus (preference for studying history or for having cats as pets) or broad focus (values such as those pertaining to honesty or sanctity of life).

    c) Motor Skill - a learned capability involving the ability to control muscular movements (e.g., riding a bicycle, printing a letter 'M', or dissecting a frog).

    d) Verbal knowledge that is frequently used or that directly supports other learnings must be well learned to assure efficient human functioning. For example, knowing the multiplication tables is useful in daily life and also basic to many other skills.

    e) (1) General knowledge facilitates socialization and effective functioning of members of a society.
        (2) It also seems to be a critical element in creative thought and in synthesis.

    f) (1) The performance involves stating a relationship in the form of a proposition (either orally or in writing).

        (2) Attitudes are expressed when we choose among alternative courses of action, thereby revealing our preferences or true values/feelings.

        (3) Motor skills performance is a physical response requiring precise organization and careful sequencing of muscular activity.

g) (1) Internal conditions for learning facts and organized knowledge - (a) have available a related, organized body of knowledge; (b) access related network of previously learned and organized propositions; (c) relate new fact(s) to an existing network and new organized knowledge to a familiar context provided by a broader knowledge structure (schema).

External conditions for learning facts - (a) present relevant context (organized knowledge) via verbal or pictorial communication; (b) present fact with suggestions for how it is to be connected to existing knowledge; (c) facilitate retention by use of imagery and elaboration; (d) provide for rehearsal by using spaced review.

External conditions for learning organized knowledge - (a)provide meaningful context (advance organizer); (b)enhance distinctiveness of cues for retrieval either visually or with auditory cues; (c) provide related information to stimulate elaboration; (d) establish in learner appropriate attention strategies or set and; (e) ensure adequate rehearsal through spaced review.

(2) Internal conditions for attitude learning - (a) respect for and/or identification with model; (b) relevant information and intellectual skills (generally concepts and rules).

External conditions for attitude learning - (a) present a credible model (need not be live mode; b) access relevant information regarding choice situation; (c)use model to demonstrate desired behavior; (d) assure vicarious reinforcement for learner/observer by identifying rewards to model from showing desired behavio; (e) reinforce learner's expression of desired attitude.

(3) Internal conditions for motor skills learning - (a) retrieve or internalize executive subroutine governing sequence of steps in the motor skill; (b) retrieve or learn pertinent part skills or response chains.

External conditions for motor skills learning - (a) demonstrate motor skill (live or film model, pictures or diagrams; (b) present appropriate verbal instructions; (c) provide opportunity for practice; (d) give informative feedback; (e) continue spaced practice to achieve automaticity of response.

2A.				2B.			
1. A	6. A	11. V		1. A	6. MS	11. VI
2. VI	7. MS	12. A		2. MS	7. VI	12. MS
3. MS	8. A	13. VI		3. VI	8. A	13. VI
4. A	9. VI	14. MS		4. MS	9. A	14. MS
5. VI	10. MS	15. VI		5. VI	10. MS	15. A

2C.					
1. DC	6. A	11. CS	16. PS	21. D	26. D
2. MS	7. MS	12. R	17. DC	22. R	27. A
3. CS	8. D	13. CC	18. CS	23. CC	
4. PS	9. CC	14. VI	19. VI	24. PS	
5. R	10. VI	15. MS	20. A	25. DC	

Feedback Matrices

Matrix for 6a

Attitudes	1	4	6	8	12
Verbal Information	2	5	9	13	15
Motor Skills	3	7	10	11	14

Matrix for 6b

Attitudes	1	6	8	9	15
Verbal Information	3	5	7	11	13
Motor Skills	2	4	10	12	14

Matrix for 6c

Attitudes	6	20	27
Verbal Information	10	14	19
Motor Skills	2	7	15
Discriminations	8	21	26
Concrete Concepts	9	13	23
Defined Concepts	1	17	25
Rules	5	12	2
Problem Solving	4	16	24
Cognitive Strategy	3	11	18

Criteria for Evaluating the Application Exercises:

1. Are the types of learning identified accurately classified?

2. Do the learnings selected adequately represent the number and types of learnings contained in the instructional material reviewed?

Examples of possible answers for a unit on earth science in an elementary school science curriculum.

Concrete concepts: minerals, rocks, fossil, mountains, plains, deserts, clouds, iceberg, glacier, volcano

Defined concepts: minerals, hardness, luster, igneous rocks, sedimentary rocks, plankton, metamorphic rocks, fossil, iceberg, glacier, desert, precipitation, water cycle, mummification

Rules: Water freezes at 0 degrees Celsius (32 degrees Fahrenheit).
Water will boil at 100 degrees Celsius (212 degrees Fahrenheit).
Dew and clouds are formed when water vapor condenses.
The rate at which igneous rocks cool affects their structural properties.

Verbal Information: Physical properties of minerals are: magnetism, appearance, hardness, streak, luster and crystals.
Three classifications of rocks are igneous, sedimentary and metamorphic.
Fossils are formed by freeezing, being petrified, mummification, being covered by sediment and by the process of hardening in tree sap.
Three-fourths of the Earth's surface is covered by water.
The five oceans are the Pacific, Atlantic, Indian, Arctic and Antarctic.
Snow is formed by freezing water vapor.
Dew and clouds are formed when water vapor condenses.

Higher-order rule: Students use experimental methods to discover the boiling/freezing points of common liquids.
Students generate a rule for determining the time required to reach the boiling point of water at different elevations.

THE LEARNER

Overview:

Although most design experts talk about adapting the instruction to the characteristics of the learner, it is not clear, beyond ascertaining the learner's entry skills, which learner characteristics are of significant importance in influencing instructional strategies.

Educational psychologist John Carroll studied factors that make a difference in what an individual will learn. From his studies he developed a model called the school learning model. Simply stated this model suggests that what an individual learns is a function of how much time he or she spends with regard to how much time he or she needs to learn a particular skill. In other words:

$$\text{Degree of Learning} = \frac{\text{Time Spent}}{\text{Time Needed}}$$

Carroll further broke down the factors that influenced the time spent by a student and the time needed. He found that the time spent is based on how much time is allowed by the instructional situation and the learner's perseverance in studying. Time needed is affected by the learner's aptitude for the subject, general intelligence, and quality of the instruction. If we equate aptitude with prior learning, and general intelligence with cognitive strategies possessed by the learner, we might begin to see that the only manipulable factors are the quality of the instruction, the mode of instruction and, perhaps, extrinsic motivation. Although this model is not discussed directly in the text, it can serve as a foundation for considering learner differences.

When you read this chapter concentrate on the role of media in allowing more time to learn. Also think about learner motivation and how it affects perseverance. What internal and external motivation factors affect the amount of time a student spends studying? Finally, how does the student's present level of knowledge affect what he or she learns in the future? What roles are played by the learning skills (cognitive strategies), and aptitude? What role does the home environment play?

Objectives:

1. **When asked in the form of an oral or written question, state:**

   a) three suggestions for considering learner characteristics during the design of instruction.

   b) two learner characteristics that are probably determined by genetics that most likely affect the design of instruction.

   c) in your own words, and give an example of the following:
   (1) schema
   (2) abilities
   (3) traits.

   d) which learner factors seem to be most important in the acquisition of new skills for each of the following types of learning outcomes:
   (1) verbal information
   (2) attitude

      (3) intellectual skills
      (4) cognitive strategies
      (5) motor skills

2. ***Given the information presented in the text, generate*** a brief hypothesis about how schema, abilities or traits could affect the design of instruction.

3. ***Given a description of an educational practice, generate*** a possible rationale for that practice, based on what you know about learner characteristics (e.g., the rationale for showing a film before beginning a new topic in class).

Practice Exercises:

1.   a) Summarize, in your own words, three considerations that the text suggests when designing instruction around learner characteristics.

     (1)

     (2)

     (3)

  b) Give an example of two learner characteristics that are probably genetic and that might affect design considerations.

     (1)

     (2)

  c) (1) Define the term "schema," and give an example of a schema.

     (2) Define the term "ability," and give an example of an ability.

(3) Define the term "trait," and give an example of a trait.

d) What learner characteristics might be important in the learning of new:

(1) verbal information

(2) intellectual skills

(3) cognitive strategies

(4) motor skills

(5) attitude

2. Explain how one of the learner characteristics (schema, abilities or traits) might affect instructional design.

3. a) Mrs. Miller plans to show portions of the film *The Last Emperor* before beginning a high school history unit on China. Hypothesize how her practice might affect verbal information learning from her subsequent lessons.

   b) Ms. Gasbard has the children tell a story about their favorite animal before beginning a science lesson on animals. In what way might this facilitate learning?

Application Exercises: (Choose two of the following exercises)

1. Form a study group in some course you have with another student in the class. Discuss the following:
   a) your respective aptitudes for the subject in terms of previous courses, practical experience or related special interests
   b) attraction to the subject content
   c) time you spend studying the subject
   d) what motivates you to study in general, and in particular with regard to this subject (both internal and external factors)
   e) what the teacher of the course could do to either reduce the time it would take you to learn, or to increase the time allowed for learning

2. Have the teacher or another student put a list of 10 numbers (1-10) and 10 objects on the blackboard
   E.g.,
   > 1 - gun
   > 2 - shoe
   > 3 - iron
   > 4 - door

   Take 5 minutes to memorize the list. Erase the list from the board and ask those who memorized it to elaborate on the strategies they used. Answer the questions in the criteria for application exercise 2 presented at the end of this chapter.

3. Brainstorm three ways that students could be given more time to learn a skill.

4. Survey any edition of *Buro's Mental Measurements Yearbook* for the description of an instrument that measures what might be a trait. What trait does it measure? How might you use information from this test in designing instruction differently from what you would design if you didn't have the information?

Feedback for Practice Exercises:

1. a) Three procedures that are necessary when designing instruction around learner characteristics are:
    (1) choosing a few of the most important characteristics of the learner population you are designing for
    (2) determining how these characteristics might affect the instructional treatment or strategies
    (3) designing first for common learner characteristics, then providing for variations that might make a difference within the target population

    b) Two learner characteristics that are probably genetic which might affect design considerations are (any two):
    (1) capacity of working memory
    (2) speed of information processing
    (3) color blindness
    (4) physical dexterity

    c) (1) Schema is a personal representation or organization of knowledge. It is hypothesized to exist as a network of propositions relating to an organizing concept, e.g., a shopping schema, a church schema, a study schema. A schema has "slots" or "nodes" to which new propositions can be attached thereby expanding the schema, or perhaps tying it to another already existing schema.

       (2) An ability is a learned skill that is relatively stable, perhaps learned early as a result of the environment, e.g., a child of musicians is likely to possess "musical ability" due to exposure to music in the family. There are also psychological abilities that seem to be developed rather than inherited, e.g., reasoning skills, verbal comprehension, number facility, spatial orientation. Since abilities generally facilitate learning it is helpful to capitalize upon them when they can be identified in a learner population.

       (3) A trait is a personality characteristic, probably learned in much the same way as an ability. Anxiety, locus of control, motivation, self-efficacy are all examples of traits. There is a line of educational research called "aptitude-treatment interaction (ATI)" that attempts to link different types of learning environments to different aptitudes or traits. Unfortunately, little information of practical value has come from this research to date.

d) How do learner characteristics affect the learning of new:

(1) <u>Verbal Information</u>
New information is best learned when it can be placed in a meaningful context of existing schema. Short of that, it is best remembered when it is meaningfully organized, and most poorly remembered when it is learned in isolation.

(2) <u>Intellectual Skills</u>
The learning of new intellectual skills depends upon recalling other prerequisite intellectual skills. Intellectual skills are hierarchical, that is, the learning of higher order skills depends upon the learning of lower order skills. Learners who do not possess the necessary prerequisite skill will experience learning difficulties.

(3) <u>Cognitive Strategies</u>
The learning of new or the development of existing strategies often depends upon prior learning. The text suggests the transfer of existing strategies from one learning problem to another is facilitated by practice. Perhaps "learning to learn" is best facilitated by practicing existing strategies on novel learning tasks.

(4) <u>Motor Skills</u>
New motor skill learning is facilitated by prior learning of part skills and verbalized information regarding performance of the skill (executive sub-routine), e.g., "Keep your head down when swinging through the golf ball." Intellectual skills may play a part when there are rules or complex procedures involved, such as a decision to pass or run on a certain defensive alignment in a football play.

(5) <u>Attitudes</u>
Attitudes are learned as expectancies or perceived benefits of choice behaviors. They can be learned as direct experiences or vicariously through the observation of others (human models). Instruction may be directed toward formulating attitudes or changing attitudes. Verbal information probably plays a big role in attitude change, but it must be delivered by a reputable model. Direct experience is probably the most effective means of changing attitudes, at least that is the belief of programs like Outward Bound. One important consideration in attitude instruction is consideration of the attitudes already held by the learners, and the source and strength of those attitudes.

2. When analyzing a learning task teachers or designers could take advantage of schema to link new learning to existing knowledge, capitalize on abilities where possible, and be aware of learner traits that they suspect may affect learning or performance of a task.

3. a) Mrs. Miller plans to show the film *The Last Emperor* before beginning a unit on the history of China. Hypothesize how her practice might affect verbal information learning with regard to learner characteristics. The film would provide a context within which to learn the new information. The visual context would be better remembered than a purely verbal one.

b) Ms. Gasbard has the children tell a story about their favorite animal before beginning a science lesson on animals. In what way might this facilitate learning? Having the students tell a story might activate a schema to which the new material to be learned can be attached.

Criteria for Evaluating the Application Exercises:

1. Did your study group find that

    a) The abilities of the members were related to their individual backgrounds?

    b) Interest in a topic was related to the degree of skill the members already had in the subject?

    c) Study times for the same subject varied among group members?

    d) Both intrinsic and extrinsic factors controlled the study times of individuals?

    e) Different members of the group have different ideas about what a teacher could do to make learning more effective, and that these ideas reflect their own abilities, traits and schema?

2. Questions to be answered regarding application exercise number 2.

    a) Was your strategy for remembering the list a general memory strategy or specific to this task?

    b) Was this a strategy that you learned at an earlier time or one you invented for this exercise?

    c) Was your strategy the same or similar to those used by others in the class?

    d) Will your strategy allow for long-term retention (24 or more hours)?

    e) Is this a strategy that you use in everyday memory tasks?

3. Considerations for application exercise number 3.

    a) Does your solution make use of mediated materials?

    b) Does your solution present alternative forms of instruction?

    c) How does your solution provide more time for learning?

    d) Does your solution take traits, schemata or abilities into consideration?

4. Criteria for Buro's task

    a) What is the test and what trait does it measure?

    b) How does this trait affect learning?

    c) How would you as a teacher or designer teach differently to persons with this trait?

NOTES

DEFINING PERFORMANCE OBJECTIVES

Overview:

The verbal information content in this chapter (objectives 1. a-h) provides a meaningful context in which to consider the attributes of performance objectives. This information establishes a rationale for the use of objectives. The major skill to be developed is the ability to write precise, unambiguous objectives which clearly communicate the learning outcomes (skills) to be acquired by the learners. Thus objectives 2 and 3 are essential prerequisites for the accomplishment of objective 4.

Objectives:

1. When asked, in the form of an oral or written question, state:

    a)   the definition of performance objective

    b)   the questions a designer needs to answer before developing instruction

    c)   the advantages of precision in defining objectives

    d)   the major limitation of course purposes and goals

    e)   the major criterion used to evaluate the precision of an objective

    f)   how a teacher/instructor can infer that a new capability has been acquired

    g)   the five components of an objective and their definitions

    h)   the learned capability verbs for each of the nine types of learning

2.   **Given a list of performance objectives, classify** the five components of each of the objectives by labeling them as situation, learned capability verb, object, action, or tools, constraints and special conditions.

3.   **Given inappropriate or incomplete examples of objectives, demonstrate** the application of the five-component format by rewriting them.

4.   **Using a curriculum guide or textbook, generate** written performance objectives in the five-component format for a chosen segment of instruction.

Practice Exercises:

1. a) Define the term performance objective.

   b) What question should a designer answer before proceeding with the development of the instruction?

   c) List two advantages of precision in objectives.
      (1)

      (2)

   d) In what way are course purposes and goals limited?

   e) What constitutes a precise objective?

   f) How can an instructor tell that a student has developed a new capability?

   g) (1) List the five components of a performance objective.
        (a)
        (b)
        (c)
        (d)
        (e)

g) (2) On the line to the left of each definition in column A, write the letter from column B for the objective component described. Each term in column B may be used once, more than once, or not at all.

Column A

Column B

___1. The stimulus faced by the learner

___2. The content of the learner's performance

___ 3. Indicates the type or domain of learning

___ 4. The observable behavior

___ 5. Limitations placed on the performance

___ 6. A description of environmental conditions under which the behavior is to be performed

___ 7. Describes how the performance is to be completed

___ 8. Helps in the application of the conditions of learning

___ 9. Subject matter

__ 10. The test environment

a. Action verb

b. Criterion of Performance

c. Learned Capability Verb

d. Object

e. Situation

f. Tools, Constraints, Special Conditions

h) On the line to the left of each of the nine types of learning, write the learned capability verb to be used in the writing of performance objectives.

_____ Discrimination

_____ Cognitive Strategy

_____ Concrete Concept

_____ Defined Concept

_____ Rule

_____ Problem Solving

_____ Attitude

_____ Motor Skill

_____ Verbal Information

2A. Label all components for each performance objective listed below. Draw one line under situation, and two lines under the learned capability verb. Box in the object, circle the action, and place a broken line under tools, constraints, or special conditions.

a) Given a list of the 50 states and a random list of all 50 capitals, the student will state the capitals by writing the number beside each state in the blank corresponding to the appropriate state capital. The student is allowed 5 minutes.

b) During a rote drill exercise in which the teacher randomly presents incomplete subtraction facts with minuends from 1-12, the student will state the number facts by responding orally and without counting. Responses must be made within 3 seconds to be judged adequate.

c) Supplied with two sticks and some dried leaves, the boy scout will execute making a fire by rubbing the sticks together. The fire must be started within 15 minutes. Matches may not be used.

d) When presented with a patient and instructions to draw a blood sample, the student will execute a venipuncture by injecting the needle into the patient's arm and withdrawing 5 ml of blood. A vacutainer and tube assembly will be used.

e) In a wood-shop class the students are presented with a mixture of different sandpaper textures. The student discriminates the textures by grouping them into similar piles.

f) A tape of different vowel sounds is played. There will be 20 pairs of sounds. The student will discriminate whether the second sound of the pair is different from the initial sound by saying "different" when the initial sound does not occur and by saying "same" when the sound does recur. Responses should be given immediately.

g) Given a set of 30 color slides, the student will identify types of white cells as neutrophils, lymphocytes, monocytes, eosinophils, and basophils by writing the name of the cell on the line corresponding to the slide number.

h) When looking at pictures of parallelograms, the student identifies squares and rectangles by placing an "S" over the squares and an "R" over the rectangles.

i) Each student is given 15 descriptions (1-3 sentences in length) of tasks completed by each of the three branches of government. Students classify executive, judicial, and legislative branch by writing E, J, or L next to each description.

j) Various life forms are described on a handout. Students will classify them as plant or animal by writing the number of the description in one of two columns labeled "plant" and "animal." No references may be used.

Classification Exercise 2B (same directions as 2A)

a) Presented with 10 problems requiring the computation of the area of trapezoids, demonstrate that the area of a trapezoid equals 1/2 (base)(height) by showing all calculations. Rule will be used from memory and the task is to be completed in 30 minutes. Calculators may not be used.

b) Given several sentences in which the nouns and verbs do not agree, demonstrate that a plural subject requires a plural verb and a singular subject requires a singular verb by crossing out the incorrect verb and writing the correct form above it.

c) Given the clinical history, blood count results, a bone marrow to review, and special stains results, the student will generate an accurate written diagnosis of the hematological disorder. The standard diagnostic form must be used.

d) Given applicant data, rating information, and a homeowner's manual, generate a complete homeowner's insurance policy in the appropriate written format.

e) Given the task of memorizing the steps in the instructional design process, adopt a method for committing them to memory within five minutes. The method chosen will be explained to the instructor.

f) Presented with research-oriented tasks, the student adopts a strategy for approaching and completing such assignments. The steps outlining this strategy will be submitted in writing to the instructor.

g) Given the opportunity to freely select foods that promote good dental health, the student chooses to eat fruits and vegetables rather than cakes, candies, and pastries during school lunch breaks.

h) When talking with colleagues and friends, the nursing student will choose to observe the confidential nature of patients' records by refraining from discussing these matters.

3. Rewrite the following objectives into the five-component format.

   SUGGESTION: First determine the type of learning; then the verb and object; next the situation for the performance; and finally any tools or constraints as required.

   a) After a lesson on parts of speech, recognize adverbs and adjectives.

   b) Plot the location of a city, given the coordinates.

   c) Write a computer program to produce mailing labels.

   d) Students in political science learn to recognize descriptions of governments as democratic or socialist.

e) Define the term "conditions of learning."

f) Given a diagram of the human ear, label each of the parts.

g) Students balance a checkbook with the aid of a calculator.

h) Select similar tastes among a variety of foods.

i) Label foods as sour or sweet.

j) Apply the rule "The product of two simple fractions is the product of the numerators divided by the product of the denominators."

k) Students in a sports class learn to spike a volleyball.

l) Identify the major battles of the Civil War.

m) Appreciate the value of reading.

n) Develop a set of attack skills for approaching case studies.

o) Write an interpretation of a political cartoon.

4. On the line to the left of each of the learned capability verbs, write the type of learning it represents.

_____	Adopt
_____	Execute
_____	Choose
_____	Generate
_____	Classify
_____	Identify
_____	Demonstrate
_____	State
_____	Discriminate

Application Exercises:

1. Obtain a curriculum guide for a course with which you are familiar. Select 10 objectives from the guide. Compare them with the five-component format. Rewrite them to fit this format. Obtain feedback from your instructor.

2. Find a textbook for a course with which you are familiar. Turn at random to a page. List the content on that page. Classify the content according to the types of learning. Write a five-component objective which clearly communicates the intended learning. Repeat the process with other pages of the text. Obtain feedback from your instructor.

Feedback For Practice Exercises:

1. a)   A precise statement of a capability that can be observed as a performance.

    b)   What will the learners be able to do after the instruction that they couldn't do before? OR How will the learner be different after the instruction.

    c)   Precision provides unambiguous communication of the intended learning outcomes, facilitates valid assessment of student performance, and assists the instructor in the evaluation of instruction.

    d)   They are not sufficiently precise for unambiguous communication of the content and outcomes of instruction.

    e)   An objective is precise when it communicates to another person what would have to be done to observe that a stated lesson purpose has in fact been accomplished.

    f)   An instructor can only infer that the capability has been attained through the observation of satisfactory performance by the learner on a task that employs that capability.

    g)   (1)   The five components of an objective are situation, learned capability verb, object, action, and tools, constraints, or special conditions.

         (2)   1. e   3. c   5. f   7. a   9. d
               2. d   4. a   6. e   8. c   10. e

    h)   Discriminate   Discrimination

         Identify   Concrete Concept

         Classify   Defined Concept

         Demonstrate   Rule

         Generate   Problem Solving

         Choose   Attitude

         Execute   Motor Skill

         State   Verbal Information

         Adopt   Cognitive Strategy

2A. Label all components for each performance objective listed below. Draw one line under situation, and two lines under the learned capability verb (we CAPITALIZED it). Box in the object (we used a different font), circle the action (*we italicized it*), and place a broken line under tools, constraints, or special conditions (**we used bold**).

a) Given a list of the 50 states and a random list of all 50 capitals, the student will STATE the capitals *by writing the number beside each state in the blank corresponding to the appropriate state capital.* **The student is allowed 5 minutes.**

b) During a rote drill exercise in which the teacher randomly presents incomplete subtraction facts with minuends from 1-12 the student will STATE the number facts *by responding orally and without counting.* **Responses must be made within 3 seconds to be judged adequate.**

c) Supplied with two sticks and some dried leaves, the boy scout will EXECUTE making a fire *by rubbing the sticks together.* **The fire must be started within 15 minutes. Matches may not be used.**

d) When presented with a patient and instructions to draw a blood sample, the student will EXECUTE a venipuncture *by injecting the needle into the patient's arm and withdrawing 5 ml of blood.* **The vacutainer and tube assembly will be used.**

e) In a wood-shop class the students are presented with a mixture of different sandpaper textures. The student DISCRIMINATES the textures *by grouping them into similar piles* **with less than 10% error rate.**

f) A tape of different vowel sounds is played. There will be 20 pairs of sounds. The student will DISCRIMINATE whether the second sound of the pair is different from the initial sound *by saying "different" when the initial sound does not occur and by saying "same" when the sound does recur.* **Responses should be given immediately.**

g) Given a set of 30 color slides, the student will IDENTIFY types of white cells as neutrophils, lymphocytes, monocytes, eosinophils, and basophils *by writing the name of the cell on the line corresponding to the slide number.*

h) When looking at pictures of parallelograms, the student IDENTIFIES squares and rectangles *by placing an "S" over the squares and an "R" over the rectangles.*

i) Each student is given 15 descriptions (1-3 sentences in length) of tasks completed by each of the three branches of government. Students CLASSIFY executive, judicial, and legislative branch *by writing E, J, or L next to each description.*

j) Various life forms are described on a handout. Students will CLASSIFY them as plant or animal *by writing the number of the description in one of two columns labeled "plant" and "animal."* **No references may be used.**

2B. a) Presented with 10 problems requiring the computation of the area of trapezoids, DEMON-STRATE that the area of a trapezoid equals 1/2 (base)(height) *by showing all calculations.* **Rule will be used from memory and the task is to be completed in 30 minutes. Calculators may not be used.**

b) Given several sentences in which the nouns and verbs do not agree, DEMONSTRATE that a plural subject requires a plural verb and a singular subject requires a singular verb *by crossing out the incorrect verb and writing the correct form above it.*

c) Given the clinical history, blood count results, a bone marrow to review, and special stains re-sults, the student will GENERATE an accurate diagnosis of the hematological disorder *in writing.* **The standard diagnostic form must be used.**

d) Given applicant data, rating information, and a homeowner's manual, GENERATE a complete homeowner's insurance policy **in the appropriate** *written* **format.**

e) Given the task of memorizing the steps in the instructional design process, ADOPT a method for committing them to memory **within 5 minutes.** *The method chosen will be explained to the instructor.*

f) Presented with research-oriented tasks, the student ADOPTS a strategy for approaching and completing such assignments. *The steps outlining this strategy will be submitted in writing to the instructor.*

g) Given the opportunity to freely select foods that promote good dental health, the student CHOOSES to *eat* fruits and vegetables rather than cakes, candies, and pastries **during school lunch breaks.**

h) When talking with colleagues and friends, the nursing student will CHOOSE to observe the con-fidential nature of patients' records *by refraining from discussing these matters.*

3. The following objectives are examples only. Your responses could vary in many ways... with the exception of the learned capability verb.

a) Given several sentences on a handout, classify adverbs by underlining and adjectives by cir-cling. Textbooks may not be used.

b) Given a grid map and the coordinates of eight cities, demonstrate that locations are plotted by using the horizontal and vertical grid lines. The name of each city will be written next to the coordinates (OR... you could give them the cities by name and ask them to provide the coordinates).

c) When provided with the necessary manuals, hardware, and a list of names and addresses, generate a computer program for producing mailing labels. Students will submit the program in writing and on disk as well as a set of mailing labels for the data provided.

d) Ten descriptions of the activities and beliefs of different governments are listed in a column. Students classify democratic and socialist forms of government by placing a "D" or an "S" on the line to the left of each description.

e) When asked in a short answer item to define "conditions of learning," the student states that conditions of learning are the specific and unique events that facilitate learning by writing the definition in the space provided.

f) NOTE: If the performance requires merely the memorization of a diagram, then verbal information is the expected outcome. Given a blank diagram of a human ear, state the parts by labeling the numbered parts.

   HOWEVER: If the performance requires recognition of the parts from pictures (i.e., based on physical attributes), then concrete concepts are the expected outcomes. Given slides or pictures of the external and internal views of the human ear, identify the eardrum, anvil, stirrup, hammer, Eustachian tube by writing the name next to the numbered part.

g) Each student is supplied with a sample bank statement and a checkbook ledger. The student will demonstrate that a checkbook is balanced by adding recent deposits to the statement balance, then subtracting outstanding checks, and then comparing the checkbook balance with the adjusted statement balance. All calculations must be shown on the statement. Calculators may be used.

h) Given several sweet and sour foods to taste, one of which is different, discriminate the tastes of sweet and sour by saying which food tastes different. Response must be made within 3 seconds.

i) Given several sweet and sour foods to taste, identify the sweet and sour tastes by labeling each food with its taste category.

j) Twenty pairs of simple fractions are listed on a sheet of paper. Students will demonstrate in writing that the product of two simple fractions is the product of the numerators divided by the product of the denominators. Calculators may not be used.

k) Working in teams of three on a volleyball court, execute the spiking of the volleyball by hitting the ball to the opposing court. Hands and feet may not cross the line or net. Hands may not touch the net.

l) Given a list of battles, state the major battles of the Civil War in chronological order by placing a number next to each battle in the correct sequence.

m) During free time students choose to read novels by checking them out of the reading center.

n) Given case studies to solve, adopt a strategy for developing effective solutions. Outline the approach in writing.

o) Given several political cartoons, students will generate an interpretation of the cartoon in essay form.

4.
COGNITIVE STRATEGY	Adopt
MOTOR SKILL	Execute
ATTITUDE	Choose
PROBLEM SOLVING	Generate
DEFINED CONCEPT	Classify
CONCRETE CONCEPT	Identify
RULE USING	Demonstrate
VERBAL INFORMATION	State
DISCRIMINATION	Discriminate

Criteria for Evaluating the Application Exercises:

1. Is the content correctly classified by type of learning?

2. Does the learned capability verb match the type of learning?

3. Does the object specify the content precisely?
   (E.g., identify roots, stem, leaves, flower rather than identify the parts of the plant.)

4. Does the situation specify performance conditions rather than instruction?

5. Is the action reasonable for the content and type of learning?

6. Are tools, constraints, or special conditions appropriate for the content and type of learning?

Examples of a Application Exercise:

EXAMPLE 1. Objectives from a curriculum guide.

(Language Arts)

1. Recognize common nouns and proper nouns. (DC)

   Given several sentences in paragraph form, classify common nouns and proper nouns by writing C or P below the nouns.

2. Know the difference between sentences and fragments. (VI, DC)

   a. On a completion exercise, state that a sentence contains a complete thought by filling in the blank.

   b. Given a list of sentences and fragments, classify sentences by labeling them with an S.

3. Use correct end punctuation. (Rules)

   A variety of types of sentences is provided. Demonstrate that a period is placed at the end of a declarative sentence by placing the appropriate end mark in the blank at the end of each sentence. (Note: A similar pattern would be used for interrogative and exclamatory sentences.)

4. Form the plurals of nouns. (Rules)

   a) Given a variety of nouns, demonstrate that singular nouns ending in -ch, -ss, -sh, or -x, add -es to form the plural. Each noun must be rewritten on the lines provided.

   b) Given a variety of nouns, demonstrate that singular nouns ending in a "y" preceded by a consonant change the "y" to "i" and add "es". Write the plurals in the blanks provided.

   (Note: Similar patterns will be used for other rules.)

5. Write the possessive forms of nouns.

   a) Given several singular phrases (e.g., the bike owned by the boy), demonstrate that singular nouns add 's to form the possessive. Each phrase is to be rewritten on the lines provided.

   b) Given several plural phrases (e.g., the children of the ladies), demonstrate that plural nouns ending in "s" add an apostrophe after the "s" to form the possessive.

EXAMPLE 2. Random content from a textbook (Elementary Science)

1. Clouds (concrete concepts)

   Twenty slides of a variety of clouds are shown to the class. Students identify cumulus, stratus, cirrus, and nimbus clouds by writing the name of the cloud next to the corresponding number on a sheet of paper.

2. Mammals (defined concept)

   Given written descriptions of real or imaginary animals, classify mammal by labeling the correct descriptions with M.

3. Thermometers (rule, concrete concept, verbal information, motor skill)

   a) Illustrations of thermometers with various temperatures are presented. Students demonstrate reading the thermometer by recording the temperature beneath each illustration.

   b) When presented with a variety of instruments, identify thermometer by labeling.

   c) On a completion item, state that thermometers measure temperature by filling in the blank.

   d) Using an oral thermometer and a classmate, execute the procedure for measuring a person's temperature.

ANALYSIS OF THE LEARNING TASK

Overview:

Chapter 8 deals with two forms of task analysis: information-processing analysis and, learning-task analysis. Task analysis is important to you as a designer because it provides a basis necessary for determining which skills need to be learned, and subsequently for providing the conditions necessary for effective instruction.

Information-processing analysis (procedural analysis) and learning-task analysis are somewhat different in their purposes. Information-processing analysis is used to describe the steps or procedures that must be learned to perform a stated skill. Learning-task analysis involves the analysis of the target skill into its enabling objectives based on principles of hierarchical skills structure and essential relationships among objectives.

In this workbook chapter, you will have a chance to practice generating a learning hierarchy task analysis, and an instructional curriculum map.

Objectives:

1. **When asked, in the form of an oral or written question, state:**

   a) the key question a designer must keep in mind when doing a task analysis

   b) the definitions, in your own words, of the following terms: target objective, enabling objective, course purpose statement, procedural task analysis, learning task analysis, prerequisite skill, essential prerequisite, supportive prerequisite, learning hierarchy

   c) the reasons why two kinds of information resulting from a procedural analysis are especially useful to instructional designers

   d) the relationship between the "steps" of an information-processing analysis and the "subordinate skills" of a learning hierarchy

   e) the relationship between a target objective and a subordinate skill by recalling a question used to derive the subordinate skill

   f) why cognitive strategies aid intellectual skill learning by writing an explanation in your own words

   g) the purpose of an instructional curriculum map in writing

   h) how verbal information objectives differ from intellectual skills when learning an upper-level intellectual skill

2. **Given descriptions of essential prerequisites, classify** the learning outcomes of these prerequisites by writing the name of the outcome next to the description.

3. **Given descriptions of supportive prerequisites, classify** the learning outcomes of these prerequisites by writing the name of the outcome next to the description.

4. **Starting with an intellectual skill target objective which you define, generate** a learning hierarchy by writing and drawing on paper.

5. **Starting with an intellectual skill target objective which you define, generate** an instructional curriculum map by writing and drawing on paper.

Practice Exercise:

Answer the following questions which were derived from the objectives.

1. a) What key question is the designer trying to answer while doing a task analysis?

   b) (1) What are target objectives?

   (2) What are enabling objectives?

   (3) In relation to the student, what does the course purpose statement describe?

   (4) List and describe the two major types of task analysis.

(5) What is a prerequisite skill?

(6) What is the difference between an essential prerequisite and a supportive prerequisite?

(7) What is a learning hierarchy?

c) What two kinds of information resulting from a procedural analysis are useful to instructional designers? Why?

d) What is the distinction between the "steps" of an information-processing analysis and the "subordinate skills" of a learning task analysis?

e) What question should a designer ask himself to derive the subordinate skills of an intellectual skill?

f)   How may cognitive strategies be used to aid intellectual skill learning?

g)   What is an instructional curriculum map? How does it differ from an intellectual skills hierarchy?

h)   How do verbal information objectives contrast with intellectual skills as prerequisites for the acquisition of an upper-level intellectual skill?

2.   Each of the behaviors below represents a prerequisite for another type of behavior. **Classify the type of outcome for which the activity is an essential prerequisite** by selecting one of the following learning outcomes : (IS) intellectual skill; (CS) cognitive strategy; (VI) verbal information; (A) attitudes; (MS) motor skill.

_____ stating the procedure for changing the blade on a chain saw

_____ learning the advantages and disadvantages of a certain technique for teaching disadvantaged children before volunteering to tutor them

_____ using the game of Monopoly to explain economic laws of supply and demand

_____ learning Spanish grammar before writing sentences

_____ watching a film on the Civil War before memorizing dates of major battles

3.   Each of the skills below represents a supportive prerequisite for other types of learning outcomes. **Classify each as the type of learning outcome** it represents: (IS) intellectual skill; (CS) cognitive strategy; (VI) verbal information; (A) attitude; (MS) motor skill.

_____ recite the letters of the alphabet

_____ use an effective list memorization strategy

_____ memorize Robert's Rules of Order in order to be an effective leader

_____ talk about the advantages of a good education

_____ identify examples of known species of a particular genus before recognizing an unknown species

Application Exercises:

Task analysis is a critical skill for instructional designers to learn. Several examples of task analyses are included in Chapter 8 of Gagné, Briggs, and Wager's book. Readers are also referred to Dick and Carey (1985). Instructional curriculum maps are shown in both these sources. Examples of a learning hierarchy and a lesson-level instructional curriculum map developed as student projects are shown on pages following the criteria for the application exercises.

1. Prepare a learning hierarchy of an intellectual skill objective which interests you. For example, if you are interested in orienteering, prepare a learning hierarchy which breaks down a target skill associated with that subject. In constructing a learning hierarchy, ask yourself, "What skills must a student acquire, the absence of which would make the target skill impossible to perform?"

2. Using the learning hierarchy you constructed in exercise 2 as a base, prepare an instructional curriculum map. Include other domains of learning which interact with intellectual skills to attain the target skill.

Feedback for Practice Exercises:

1. a) Instructional designers should ask themselves, "What will students be doing after they have learned?"

    b) (1) Target objectives are those objectives to be attained at the end of a course of study.

        (2) Enabling objectives are prerequisites of target objectives -- those that are attained during a course of study.

        (3) The course purpose statement should be concerned with what a student should be able to do after a course of study.

        (4) (a) Information-processing or procedural task analysis: describes the steps in the sequence of performing a task or skill. The sequence includes choice and alternative actions.
        (b) Learning task analysis: identifies the skills necessary to perform each step of the information-processing analysis. The learning task analysis may uncover objectives which are not taught in the information-processing analysis, but which are required to transfer the newly learned skill to other problems.

        (5) A prerequisite skill is learned prior to the target skill and enables the learning of the target objective.

        (6) An essential prerequisite is a component skill that must be learned before completely learning a target skill. A supportive prerequisite may be helpful in learning a target objective quicker or with less effort, but is not absolutely required.

(7) A learning hierarchy is the product of a learning task analysis for intellectual skills. It displays the target skill broken down into successively simpler skills.

c) (1) A flow chart makes it possible to specify the presentation sequence of the target performance.

(2) The revelation of steps which require internal processing as well as overt behavior is important in specifying the steps of the procedure.

d) The "steps" of an information-processing analysis are what an individual does in exhibiting a target performance which may be assumed to have been learned previously. "Subordinate skills" of a learning task analysis are those skills that an individual must learn in sequence from the simplest to the most complex.

e) For a given target objective, a designer should ask himself a question similar to the following: "What simpler intellectual skill or skills would a learner have to acquire to learn this target objective?"

f) Cognitive strategies may help in learning intellectual skills faster. Also, they may make intellectual skills easier to remember or aid in generalizing to novel instances.

g) An instructional curriculum map indicates the functional relationships among both essential and supportive instructional objectives. It differs from an instructional skills hierarchy in that it contains objectives from many different domains of learning (as opposed to objectives from only the intellectual skills domain).

h) Verbal information objectives may be very useful as supportive objectives for intellectual skill learning, but research does not support their use as essential prerequisites. In contrast, subordinate intellectual skills are essential for learning upper-level intellectual skills.

2. (MS) motor skills
   (A) attitudes
   (CS) cognitive strategies
   (IS) intellectual skills
   (VI) verbal information

3. (VI) verbal information
   (CS) cognitive strategies
   (A) attitudes
   (MS) motor skills
   (IS) intellectual skills

Criteria for Evaluating the Application Exercises:

1. Learning Hierarchy Criteria

    *   Did you work backwards from the target skill in order to reveal simpler components which make it possible for the learner to master the target skill?

    *   Does every rule break down to at least two other rules, a rule and concept, or two other concepts?

    *   Do concepts consist of simpler concepts or discriminations?

    *   Are all objectives in the learning hierarchy intellectual skills?

    *   Is the target skill broken down into successively simpler steps?

2. Instructional Map Criteria

    *   Is the map identified as a course, unit or lesson map?

    *   Are the relationships among the objectives in the map supportive? (Do the lower level skills support learning the higher level skills? Do objectives from a different domain support objectives coming later in sequence?)

    *   Have you shown verbal information objectives which support the intellectual skills?

    *   What attitudes are functionally related to the intellectual skill target objective?

    *   Are there motor skills which may be used to facilitate learning of the target skill or can they be ignored?

    *   Have you diagrammed domain changes in ways which indicate functional relationships among all the objectives.

An example of a learning hierarchy from a student project by Ed Lagman

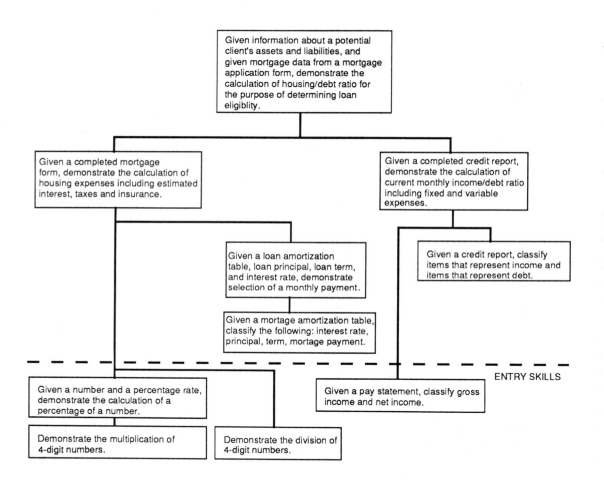

An example of an instructional curriculum map from a student project by Dave Proulx

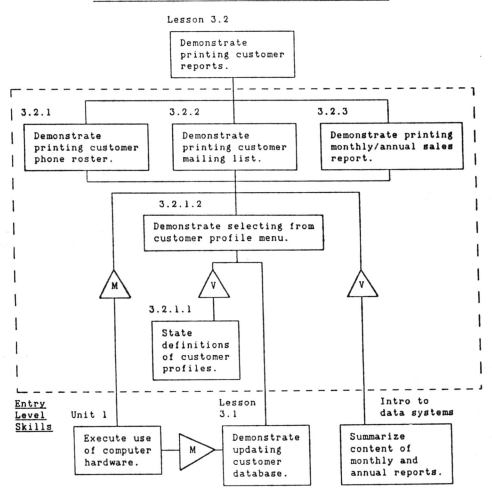

COURSE TITLE: Fundamentals of Office Automation

NOTES

DESIGNING INSTRUCTIONAL SEQUENCES

Overview:

This chapter describes sequencing considerations that must be made when designing a course. A top-down approach helps the designer to think of the highest level objectives first, and the subordinate objectives for achieving the higher level objectives next. The problem in course design is dividing the task into manageable chunks. One technique for deriving objectives from a content outline (Tyler technique) is illustrated. A second technique of Instructional Curriculum Mapping illustrates how a succession of increasingly detailed maps, from the course to the lesson level, can be used to diagram the relationships among instructional objectives. You are encouraged to do the exercises described in this workbook to get a feel for how the model can be employed.

The application exercises in this chapter can take a fair amount of time, especially if you have never done this before. Use the examples in the text and in the workbook as models for your instructional curriculum maps.

Objectives:

1. When presented with an oral or written question, state:

   a) the definitions of five different levels of course objectives (lifelong, course, unit, specific, enabling)

   b) the definition of top-down analysis

   c) briefly, the concepts of an epitome and an elaboration in component display theory

   d) a description of the Ralph Tyler approach for defining objectives from topical units

   e) the rule of sequencing within the intellectual skills domain of learning outcomes

2. Given five different objectives taken from different levels of a course, categorize objectives into one of five levels (lifelong, Course, Unit, Specific, Enabling).

3. Using a top-down approach, demonstrate the construction of a course level map that contains at least three units for a course you could teach. (See Figure 9-1 in text.)

4. Given a course map, demonstrate application of a top-down approach by constructing a unit level ICM.

5. Given a unit level ICM, demonstrate application of a top-down approach by constructing a lesson- level ICM, showing target skills and entry skills.

6. Given a lesson level ICM, demonstrate the use of hierarchical sequencing rules by numbering the objectives in the order in which they should be taught, with an explanation for your sequence.

Practice Exercises:

1. a) Define the five different levels of course objectives.
        (1)

        (2)

        (3)

        (4)

        (5)

    b) What is meant by the term "top-down" analysis?

    c) What is an epitome and an elaboration, according to component display theory?

    d) Summarize Ralph Tyler's approach to defining objectives for topical units.

2. a) Classify each of the following as LL (lifelong objective), CO (course objective), UO (unit objective), SO (specific objective), EO (enabling objective).

    ___ (1) The student will state the definition of electoral votes.
    ___ (2) The student will summarize how the popular and electoral votes differ.
    ___ (3) The student will classify, by example, the function of the electoral college.
    ___ (4) The student will demonstrate, by writing a scenario, how a president may win the popular vote but lose an election.
    ___ (5) The student will be an informed future voter.

   b) Write an objective at each level for a course you might teach:

lifelong Objective

Course Objective

Unit Objective

Specific Objective

Enabling Objective

Application Exercises:

1. Choose a course that you might teach and describe it in terms of the major course purpose, the intended audience, the significance of the course, and the timeframe in which it is to be taught. Include reference to lifelong and end-of-course objectives (although they need not be formally stated).

2. Construct a course level map that contains at least three major unit objectives (see Figure 9-1 in text).

5. Choose one of the units from this map and construct a unit map (see Figure 9-2).

6. Demonstrate division of the unit into lessons (see Figure 9-3).

7. Demonstrate the use of sequencing rules for objectives within a lesson by numbering the objectives in a unit and lesson map and giving a justification of the sequence chosen.

Feedback for Practice Exercises:

1. a) Define the five different levels of curriculum objectives.

    (1) Lifelong Objectives - broader goals that are served as a function of the course

    (2) End-of-Course Objectives -highest level performance outcomes expected at the end of the course

    (3) Unit objectives - major outcomes of topical units within the course

    (4) Specific performance objectives - generally intellectual skill and attitude outcomes at the lesson level

    (5) Enabling objectives - essential or supportive prerequisites for lesson objectives

    b) What is meant by the term "top-down" analysis? Starting with the terminal behavior and asking "What must a person know in order to be able to learn this skill?"

    c) What is the sequencing relationship between an epitome and an elaboration, according to component display theory? An epitome is a generalization, perhaps the statement of a rule, or the definition of a concept. An elaboration is more detail, perhaps examples of the rule or concept focusing on relevant procedure or relationships among the attributes of a concept.

    d) Tyler's approach is to list the topics that would be covered in a course, and then ask, "What should the learner be able to do after studying these topics?" We have elaborated on Tyler's method by asking, "What attitudes, intellectual skills, verbal information, motor skills and/or cognitive strategies should the learner gain from this topical unit?"

    e) The sequencing rule for intellectual skills is that you should teach all the subordinate rules for a particular skill before teaching the skill. In this sense, discriminations are taught before concepts, concepts are taught before rules, and rules before problem solving.

2. a) Classify each of the following as LL (lifelong objective), CO (course objective), UO (unit objective), SO (specific objective), EO (enabling objective).

     EO   The student will state the definition of electoral votes.
     SO   The student will summarize how the popular and electoral votes differ.
     UO   The student will classify, by example, the function of the electoral college.
     CO   The student will demonstrate, by writing a scenario, how a president may win the popular vote but lose an election.
     LL   The student will be an informed future voter.

   b) Write an objective for each level from a course you might teach, e.g.,
     LL   The student will choose to learn more about instructional design.
     CO   The student will demonstrate the use of a design model.
     UO   The student will demonstrate construction of five component objectives.
     LO   The student will classify different types of learning outcomes.
     SO   The student will state the nine learned capability verbs.

Criteria for the Application Exercises:

1. The descriptions emphasize course goals or outcomes rather than process.

2. The rationale for the course reflects a recognition of need.

3. The course goal or outcome is measurable.

4. The course level map shows a unit structure that contains objectives subordinate to the course objective(s).

5. The unit level objectives are all measurable, and are identified according to the type of learning outcome they represent.

6. The objectives in the unit map are subordinate to the unit objective and are represented as required or supportive prerequisites.

7. The sequencing of intellectual skills follows the rules for hierarchical relationships.

8. The unit is broken down into lessons that can be completed in from 30 to 60 minutes. The sequence for each lesson is easily discernible from the numbering system used.

9. Objectives from two or more domains are represented in the unit map.

10. Both maps are neatly presented and easy to follow.

Student example of the application exercises by Greg Stevens:

<u>Course Title</u>: Basic Job Search Techniques

Description: This course is intended for college juniors and seniors who are preparing to conduct a job search for a position following graduation. Taught in the course are those skills that will increase the students' chances of a successful job search as determined by a higher job offer acceptance rate by students completing the course than those who do not. The course includes the preparation of a personal inventory, a resumé, and correspondence for prospective employment situations. Students will demonstrate effective interviewing skills.

It is anticipated that the course would be approximately 15 hours of instruction, spread over 10 weeks. Successful completion is contingent upon the learner mastering the skills in all five units.

<u>Lifelong objective</u>: The learner will apply effective job search techniques to the task of securing employment.

<u>End-of-Course Objective</u>: The learner will generate a job search plan including: preparation of a personal inventory, a resumé, and a cover letter, identification of prospective employers and positions, and demonstration of basic interviewing skills.

<u>Unit objectives</u>:
Unit One: Preparing a personal inventory - Starting with his transcript and list of employment experiences the student will demonstrate the construction of a personal job skills inventory that capitalizes on his or her strengths, and desired direction of employment, by listing those skills under topical headings.

Unit Two: Preparing a resumé - Starting with a given set of resumé information, the student will demonstrate the organization of that information into both chronological and functional formats, and present it in an appropriate prose or outline style.

Unit Three: Identifying Potential Positions - The learner will demonstrate the selection of five positions that are in alignment with his or her personal inventory by listing the positions, their skill requirements and the match with the inventory.

Unit Four: Employer Correspondence - The learner will generate cover letters and completed job applications for positions selected in unit three that are customized with regard to job requirements and personal skills.

Unit Five: Interview Skills - The learner will demonstrate and execute both nonverbal and verbal interview skills and techniques.

<u>Suggested sequence for the units</u>:
As indicated on the course level map, the presentation of the units does not have to follow the numerical sequence of the units. However, since learning in some of the units can take advantage of products produced in other units, some units are more logically presented before others. The units follow in the order of the steps that would typically be followed in the process of a job search.

Example of a Course Level Map by Greg Stevens

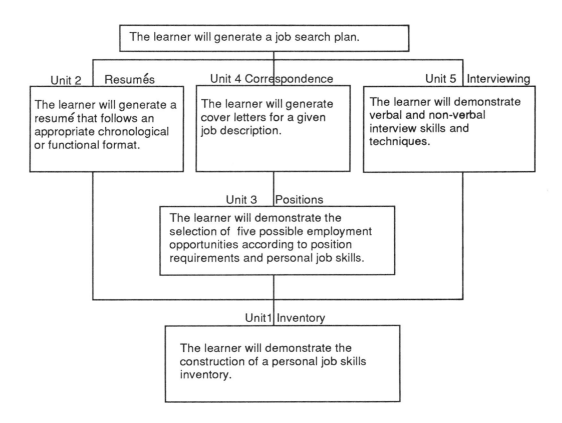

Example of a Unit Level Map by Greg Stevens

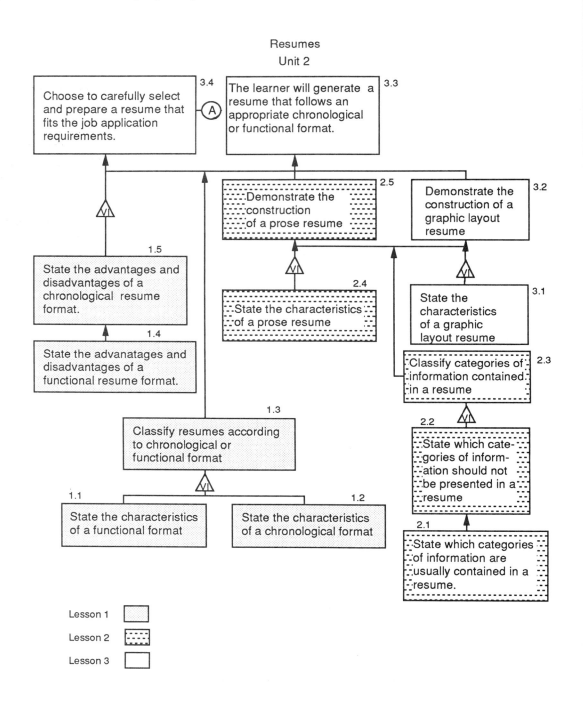

Resumes
Unit 2

3.4 — Choose to carefully select and prepare a resume that fits the job application requirements.

(A)

3.3 — The learner will generate a resume that follows an appropriate chronological or functional format.

2.5 — Demonstrate the construction of a prose resume

3.2 — Demonstrate the construction of a graphic layout resume

1.5 — State the advantages and disadvantages of a chronological resume format.

2.4 — State the characteristics of a prose resume

3.1 — State the characteristics of a graphic layout resume

1.4 — State the advanatages and disadvantages of a functional resume format.

2.3 — Classify categories of information contained in a resume

1.3 — Classify resumes according to chronological or functional format

2.2 — State which categories of information should not be presented in a resume

1.1 — State the characteristics of a functional format

1.2 — State the characteristics of a chronological format

2.1 — State which categories of information are usually contained in a resume.

Lesson 1
Lesson 2
Lesson 3

EVENTS OF INSTRUCTION

Overview:

This chapter presents one of the most important concepts in the text, the process of instruction. It seeks to answer the question, "How does one instruct the learner?" Instruction is seen as a series of external events that promote (facilitate) internal information processing, and therefore learning.

The events of instruction are extremely practical for the instructor or the instructional designer because they can serve as a guide for what to do. Learning activities, such as field trips, can be thought of as groups of events that serve some purpose in the learning process. By analyzing a particular learning activity for the events of instruction it presents, a teacher or designer can see what additional activities might be needed to make instruction effective.

The exercises in this chapter call for recall of basic information about the events of instruction. Additional discussion of the events of instruction will follow in chapters 11, 12, 14, and 15. Use the practice exercises to check the accuracy of your definitions. There are several matching exercises of increasing difficulty requiring you to analyze teaching behavior with respect to the events of instruction they present. Application exercise 3 provides an opportunity for you to practice applying the events of instruction to a lesson you design.

Objectives:

1. **When asked, in the form of an oral or written question, state:**

    a) a definition of instruction

    b) the derivation of the events of instruction

    c) a useful way of thinking about or describing the events of instruction

    d) implications of this view for teacher talk and for using media

    e) the relationship between self-instruction and the events of instruction

    f) the internal learning processes involved in a single act of learning

    g) definitions of each of the nine events of instruction

    h) the learning processes activated by each event of instruction

2. **Given a list of teacher activities, classify** each activity by matching it to the name of the event of instruction it represents.

3. **Given abbreviated lesson segments, classify** the segments by matching each to the event of instruction it represents.

4. **Given lesson activities in random order, classify** each activity with regard to the event of instruction it most likely represents.

5. **In a live or filmed classroom situation, classify** instances of the events of instruction when they are observed being exhibited by teachers.

6. **Given the task of writing a lesson that teaches a single objective, generate** a lesson plan that incorporates the appropriate use of each event of instruction.

Practice Exercises:

1. a) What is the definition of instruction presented in your text?

    b) What is the basis or derivation of the instructional events that Gagné identified?

    c) What is a useful way of explaining the meaning of the events of instruction?

    d) What implications does this view of instruction have for teacher talk? Media Selection?

    e) Explain how the events of instruction are related to self-instruction.

    f) Name the kinds of internal processing that are believed to occur during any act of learning.

g) Describe the physical structures and the sequence of processing that is postulated to occur during learning.

h) Write a definition of each event of instruction. Also list the learning process(es) activated by each event of instruction.

(1)

(2)

(3)

(4)

(5)

(6)

(7)

(8)

(9)

General Directions for exercises 2-4.

The exercises that follow provide practice in recognizing instances of the events as they might occur in ordinary instructional activities. While the description of teacher behavior varies in detail and context, you should be able to classify the activity as representative of at least one of the events of instruction. Check your answers after each exercise. The events and their numbers are:

1. gaining attention,
2. informing learner of objective,
3. stimulating recall of prior learning,
4. presenting stimulus material,
5. providing learning guidance,
6. eliciting performance,
7. providing feedback,
8. assessing performance,
9. enhancing retention and transfer.

2. This matching exercise presents descriptions of different teaching behaviors. Select the event of instruction that would most likely be accomplished by that behavior and write the number of that event in the space. All events will be used at least twice.

____ a) asking questions about topics related to new learning

____ b) making a specific reading assignment for class

____ c) changing voice level

____ d) prompting students when necessary

____ e) giving a 10 minute lecture

____ f) informing learner of adequacy of his/her response

____ g) providing periodic review of prior learnings

____ h) showing examples of expected performance

____ i) providing practice activities/materials

____ j) initiating a class by asking leading questions

____ k) providing summary (example and brief explanation) of rule just taught

____ l) describing intended learning to students

____ m) asking student(s) to respond to oral questions

____ n) using a transparency to give an example of a concept or rule

____ o) using an objective test to measure learning

___ p) requiring performance on similar tasks involving diverse content

___ q) sequencing task into manageable steps

___ r) providing answer keys in text

___ s) giving students several problems to be solved

___ t) giving a brief review of the past unit's concepts

___ u) suggesting a rhyme to help learn a rule

3. The next three classification exercises consist of lesson plans divided into segments. Each lesson is designed to teach one objective and each segment occurs in the order in which it would be presented in the lesson. Select the event of instruction that matches each lesson segment and write the number of that event in the space provided. All of the events will be used at least once. Some lesson segments contain two events. Also note that some lesson segments for objectives B and C represent only one part of a series of communications to the learner that are designed to achieve a particular event of instruction. Do the exercise for objective A, check your answers. For additional practice do exercises B and C.

Objective A: <u>Students are presented with clock faces showing various examples of 5-minute intervals.   They demonstrate the rule for determining time (in 5-minute intervals) by writing the time in the space provided below each clock.</u>

___ a) "Who can tell me what time we eat lunch?" (Student responds11:15.) Call students' attention to the transparency clock face displayed on the overhead projector. "If I wanted to show what time we go to lunch on this clock, where would I place the hands?"

___ b) "Today each of you will get to tell time on this clock, times like 15 minutes after 11 o'clock, 25 minutes after 1 o'clock, 35 minutes after 2 o'clock and many other times."

___ c) With the aid of the transparency clock, have volunteers identify the minute hand and the hour hand. Have someone show which way the hands move around the clock. Position the hands to show times to the hour and half-hour. Give every student the opportunity to tell the time shown. To complete this review, assign page 72 in text and correct upon completion.

___ d) Call attention to the transparency clock and have students recall that it takes 5 minutes for the minute hand to move from one numeral to the next. Have the students count by 5's as the minute hand on the demonstration clock is moved from numeral to numeral, thereby reviewing the fact that there are 60 minutes in one hour and 30 minutes in one half-hour.

___ e) Continue this review by having students complete the exercise on page 73 of their texts.

___ f) Write on the board __minutes after __ o'clock. Display the time 11:15 on the transparency clock. Have the students identify the position of the minute hand. Instruct them to begin at 1 and counting by 5's move from numeral to numeral until they arrive at the numeral where the minute hand rests. "How many minutes does this clock show?" After response, write 15 in the first blank on the board. Direct students' attention to the hour hand and ask: "What numeral does the hour hand come after?" Then fill in the second blank on the board and have students read the time on the board:15 minutes after 11 o'clock.

___g)   Show various times on the transparency clock and have a few students go to the board to fill in the blanks, __minutes after __o'clock, and read the time they write. Students performing this task correctly will be praised. Students who make mistakes will be helped to understand why their answer was wrong and be given another chance to perform.

___h)   Distribute worksheet that requires students to write the time shown by each clock without teacher guidance.

___i)   Correct worksheet; return and go over on following day.

___j)   Include 10 clock faces showing time in 5-minute intervals on one section of next unit test. Have students respond in same manner as in previous worksheet exercises.

___k)   Within a week distribute individual mini-clocks to all students. Have the students choose partners and have one child position the hands on the clock while the partner tells the time (then alternate roles). Teacher and aide will check periodically.

Objective B: <u>When presented with a number of slides or pictures of abrasions and incisions, students will identify these concepts by writing on their paper the name corresponding to each slide or picture.</u>

Lesson Activities:

__a)   "Class, I'm sure you have all had a scraped knee at one time or another. When I was a kid, I used to keep at least one knee skinned up -- usually both."

__b)   "Scraped knees are a common, minor injury. They are usually nothing to get alarmed over."

__c)   "Today we are going to talk about a couple of different types of wounds : abrasions and incisions."

__d)   "If you remember, last week we talked about puncture wounds and lacerations. Who can tell me a little bit about these types of wounds? So, if you fell on a nail and it stuck through your hand, what kind of wound would that be?"

__e)   "Incisions are usually less severe than punctures or lacerations." Teacher presents picture of an incision. "Incisions are often confused with lacerations due to their similar characteristics."

__f)   "Can anyone look at this picture of an incision and this picture of a laceration and tell me what the difference in the two is?" "Right! An incision is a neat, clean cut; a laceration is a tear which is usually very jagged. They can be big or small, painful or not."

__g)   "You've figured out what incisions are from analyzing these pictures. Let's check you out a little more carefully. Which of these three pictures of wounds is a puncture, a laceration, an incision? Correct, the first is an incision, the second a laceration and the third is a puncture."

__h) "Now we have learned to identify punctures, lacerations and incisions. There is one other type of injury I would like to present today -- abrasions. Abrasions are very easy to identify."

__i) Teacher holds up a picture of an abrasion. "From looking at this picture of an abrasion, can anyone give me a more common name for it? (Wait and give hint if necessary.) Yes, A 'strawberry'! That's what many people call it. What has happened to the skin? Exactly! The skin has been scraped off."

__j) "From this information, who can tell me what an abrasion is?" (Again teacher waits and then prompts learners to form accurate definition if theirs is incomplete.)

__k) The teacher shows slides of different wounds (lacerations, punctures, abrasions and incisions) and calls on different students to name the wound pictured in each slide.

__l) Teacher provides help if necessary. After the correct response is given, student is asked to explain his or her answer and another student is asked to evaluate the explanation.

__m) Students are given a test requiring identification of pictures of the four types of wounds that were taught. It is collected at the end of the class period and scored.

__n) Students will frequently use their knowledge of incisions and abrasions in learning other concepts to be taught in the present unit.

Objective C: <u>Given several selections of poems containing figurative language, the student will classify examples of metaphors by underlining the metaphors.</u>

Lesson Activities:

__a) Pass out copies of poems. Read poems aloud.

__b) Write the following on the board: "The Sea is a Wilderness of Waves, A Wilderness of Water." Tell the class that this is a new type of comparison and that at the end of the period they will be asked to classify examples like this one.

__c) Ask student to look again at the poems that were just read and point out examples of figurative language.

__d) Ask them to find comparisons.

__e) Ask them if there are similes in the poems.

__f) Ask also for definitions of figurative language, comparison, and simile.

__g) Say, "This is an example of a new kind of figurative language: My friend, Henry, is a fish in water."

__h) Ask how is it like a simile and how it is different?

__i) Pass out copy of a poem that contains metaphors, some underlined and some not.

__ j) Ask students if they can detect a pattern in the way the comparisons (the underlined metaphors) are made.

__ k) Prompt students by asking what things are being compared and what is their relationship.

__ l) Tell students that the comparisons they have been looking at are called metaphors.

__ m) Ask for a definition of a metaphor.

__ n) Clarify as needed and give summary definition of metaphor. Proceed with following example: "Under the moonlight, the river is a silver ribbon." Have a student identify critical attributes in this example.

__ o) Pass out other examples of poems containing metaphors and have students work in pairs underlining the metaphors in the poems.

__ p) Share answers with whole group confirming and correcting responses.

__ q) To evaluate learning, present two new poems with directions to underline the metaphors.

__ r) As other poems are read in the class later in the unit, ask students to classify examples of metaphors and similes.

4. For the matching exercise below, you are given lesson segments presented in random order for two lessons. Each lesson was designed to teach a single objective in a high school vocational education course. For each lesson segment, select the corresponding event of instruction and write the number (1-9) of the instructional event. All events occur at least once and some events occur more than once in each lesson.

Objective A: When presented slides of the tools commonly used by electricians, learners will identify each tool by writing the name on their test paper.

____ a) Presentation of actual tools.

____ b) Each tool is named by the teacher and its characteristics are discussed.

____ c) Pictures of various tools are presented; students name them.

____ d) Teacher comments briefly on pertinent tools students already know.

____ e) Teacher begins class by asking how students became interested in the vocation of electricians.

____ f) Students respond in unison as teacher holds up tools used by electricians.

____ g) Statement: "You will learn the names of all major tools used by electricians."

____ h) Video tape shows variations (different examples) of each tool.

___i) Teacher goes over a matching exercise involving the naming of pictures of tools.

___j) Students use proper tools when working on repair assignments.

___k) Slides of electricians' tools are presented; students write names of tools on their tests.

___l) Students complete matching exercise involving pictures of tools and a list of tools.

Objective B: <u>Given diagrams of six circuits where the value of the voltage, current or resistance is</u> <u>unknown, student demonstrates Ohm's law by calculating the missing value. Compu-</u> <u>tations must be shown.</u>

___a) "Six circuits are shown below. In each circuit, one of the values for voltage, current, or resis-tance is not given. Use Ohm's law and determine the unknown value."

___b) "Complete the exercises on page 26."

___c) "When you finish page 26, check your answers on page 345."

___d) "In today's lesson you will learn about a rule that gives the relationship between voltage, current and resistance. This rule is known as Ohm's law."

___e) "Now you use Ohm's law to solve this problem, 'If the current is 4 amps and the voltage is 10 volts, what is the resistance?' "

___f) "Two weeks ago you learned Ohm's law. Let's see if you still know how to use it. Compute the value of the unknown for the circuits shown below."

___g) "Is the current in a circuit directly proportional or inversely proportional to voltage? That's right, directly proportional. So, if there is a greater resistance, there will be less current. This means that current is inversely proportional to resistance or $I = V / R$. When we combine these two facts, the result is $I = V / R$, Ohm's law. It can also be written as $V = I * R$.

___h) "Let's use the formula with a problem. If the current is 6 amps and the voltage is 30 volts, what is the resistance? Ohm's law tells us that voltage(V) is equal to Current(I) times Resistance(R) or $V = I * R$. Solving for R, we find that the resistance is 5. We can also just as easily solve for missing values of I or V." Instructor works two more example problems.

___i) "Before beginning this lesson, please answer these questions about voltage(V), current (I) and resistance(R)."

___j) "Suppose specifications for a wire state that its capacity cannot exceed 20 volts. How much current could this wire support if the resistance of the wire were 2 ohms? This is one type of problem that every electrician should know how to solve."

Application Exercises:

The events of instruction must be considered whenever instruction is designed. They help guide many of the most important instructional design decisions, and they provide a set of criteria with which to evaluate any instruction regardless of form. Consequently, it is necessary to practice applying the events of instruction so as to become skillful in their use. It is also of value to practice judging which events of instruction are being employed during the course of classroom instruction, instruction from text or from other media. The following exercises are suggested for the purpose of providing a) practice in recognizing the application of the events of instruction in a variety of instructional forms and b) some initial practice in applying the events to the design of instruction where the instructional outcomes are purposely limited.

1. Take notes in one or more of your classes on the ways in which the events of instruction are accomplished. Due to the sophistication (at least assumed) of post-secondary students, you very likely will not observe all of the events being served, and certainly not in a single class period. How might instructional activities have been conducted to more adequately achieve various events of instruction (both those events addressed in the instruction you observed and those omitted from instruction)?

2. Apply the same analysis above to:
    a) a video tape of a complete lesson being taught or of a segment of micro-teaching
    b) a filmstrip
    c) instructional software
    d) programmed text

3. Construct a lesson plan (script) of the form presented in practice exercise 3 of this chapter. Begin by carefully specifying a single performance objective. Then develop a lesson that correctly incorporates each event of instruction. Also label the events of instruction as they occur in your lesson plan. Have a classmate and/or your instructor critique your lesson plan.

Feedback for Practice Exercises:

a) Instruction is a set of events external to the learner that is intended to support the internal processes of learning.

b) Gagné's events of instruction have been derived from analysis of the internal learning processes identified in cognitive learning theories (information-processing theory).

c) Think of the events of instruction as a set of communications designed to aid the process of learning.

d) Use of these events should sensitize a designer or teacher to the importance of using instructional time efficiently.

e) Self-instruction is governed by cognitive strategies which may allow the learner to provide events of instruction for him or herself. External events provided in the instruction are there to facilitate internal processing, and should help individuals who lack good learning strategies. However, providing all the events should also facilitate learning for a good learner.

f) The types of internal processing that occur during learning include:

1) attention	5) retrieval
2) selective perception	6) response organization
3) rehearsal	7) feedback
4) semantic encoding	

In addition, executive control processes operate as cognitive strategies that serve to modify any or all of the previous internal processes.

g) (1) Gaining attention - event designed to direct and stimulate learners' physical and cognitive (interests/motivation) orientation to the learning stimulus. It influences reception of patterns of neural impulses.

(2) Informing learner of the objective - communicating to the learner the performance or learning outcome desired. This event activates a process of executive control.

(3) Stimulating recall of prerequisite learning - event designed to bring pertinent prior learnings to attention of learner. This ensures retrieval of prior learning to working memory.

(4) Presenting stimulus material - content of the new learning is presented. The learning stimulus should be presented in such a way as to direct students to focus on the essential stimulus features.   This event emphasizes features of the stimulus thereby enhancing selective perception.

(5) Providing learning guidance - communications designed to aid or lead learner to make the connections involved in any new learning. External conditions of learning indicate general features of instruction that are necessary to establish learning. Elaboration on these conditions is essential to facilitating understanding. This event stimulates semantic encoding and provides cues for retrieval.

(6) Eliciting the performance - having the learner exhibit the desired learning during the course of instruction. This forces the learner to try out the new learning and gives an initial indication of the degree of learning. This event serves to activate response organization.

(7) Providing feedback - giving the learners information about the correctness of their performance; allows for correction of misconceptions. Enables reinforcement to occur.

(8) Assessing the performance - conducting valid and reliable measurement of students' mastery of learning outcomes. This event activates retrieval of new learning and makes reinforcement possible.

(9) Enhancing retention and transfer - activities involving the new learning that are designed to: a) improve future retrieval of the learning and/or b) facilitate transfer (application) of the learning to different situations from those experienced during instruction. This event can occur during instruction (through events 3, 4, 5 and 6), as well as after instruction through review, elaboration activities, or as an integral part of successive learnings.

2 .

a) 3	e) 4	i) 6	m) 6	q) 5&3	u) 5
b) 4	f) 7	j) 1	n) 4	r) 7	
c) 1	g) 9&3	k) 5&9	o) 8	s) 8&6	
d) 5	h) 2	l) 2	p) 9&6	t) 3&9	

3A.	a) 1	d) 3	g) 6&7	j) 8	
	b) 2	e) 3	h) 6	k) 9	
	c) 3	f) 4&5	i) 7		

3B.	a) 1	e) 4	i) 4&5	m)8	
	b) 1	f) 5	j) 5	n) 9	
	c) 2	g) 6	k) 6		
	d) 3	h) 2	l) 7		

3C.	a) 1	e) 3	i) 4	m)5	q) 8
	b) 2	f) 3	j) 5	n) 5	r) 9
	c) 3	g) 4	k) 5	o) 6	
	d) 3	h) 5	l) 5	p) 7	

4A.	a) 4	e) 1	i) 7	
	b) 5	f) 6	j) 9	
	c) 6	g) 2	k) 8	
	d) 3	h) 5	l) 6	

4B.	a) 8	d) 2	g) 4	j)1
	b) 6	e) 6	h) 5	
	c) 7	f) 9	i) 3	

Criteria for Evaluating the Application Exercises:

1. All events of instruction are included and used appropriately.
2. Events of instruction are repeated as necessary.
3. Assessment is valid for learning outcome designated.
4. Lesson activities incorporate the internal and external conditions of learning necessary for type of learned capability designated in performance objective.

Example of the application exercise for a lesson script designed to teach the following objective.

> Given a worksheet containing 12 descriptions of igneous and non-igneous rocks, the student will be able to classify the examples of igneous rock by marking an "I" next to the appropriate descriptive statements.

"Class, clear your desk of everything except your pencil." Distribute a few rocks among the children and then ask, "What have I passed out among you?" Gaining Attention

"That's right. They are the same rocks we identified yesterday. Today we are going to learn how some rocks are formed inside the Earth." Informing Learner of Objective

"Yesterday we learned the names of these rocks. Raise your hand if you can tell me the name of one of the rocks." As the class responds, the teacher will tell the children if they have correctly identified the rock and if not ask if anyone can name the rock. The rocks to be identified are granite, lava, sandstone, limestone, marble, and slate. Teacher holds up a lava rock and says, "Diane said this rock is a lava rock. How did she know that? She remembered what it looked like." Hold up a piece of limestone and ask, "Does this limestone look like the lava? Tell me how they are different." After asking students to make other comparisons, say that the rocks are different in appearance because of the ways in which they were formed. <u>Stimulating Recall</u>

Draw a simple volcano on the board and write the word 'igneous' beside it. "Igneous means formed from fire, and igneous rocks are formed from the hot magma inside the earth." Hold up lava rock. "This lava was formed when the hot magma reached the earth's surface. If we baked clay until it became hard as a rock, would it be considered an igneous rock?" Volunteers contribute to discussion. "Very good. That is right. In order to be considered an igneous rock, the rock has to come from deep inside the earth's surface and be formed from the "fire" or molten material inside." <u>Presenting Stimulus, Providing Learning Guidance</u>

"Why does lava look different from granite if they are both igneous rocks?" After students offer various explanations, give appropriate feedback and then explain as follows, "Some rocks cool on the surface of the earth, like lava. Other rocks, like granite, cool under the surface of the earth. It is important to understand that the way in which rocks cool determines the features that we see in different igneous rocks." <u>Providing Learning Guidance</u>

Elicit responses at this time by asking several questions such as the following and giving appropriate feedback to student and class after each response. Would a rock that had been formed from shells be an igneous rock? Would a rock formed when a volcano erupts be an igneous rock? <u>Eliciting Performance, Providing Feedback</u>

Pass out a worksheet listing the names of several rocks and brief descriptions of how they were formed. Have students place an "I" in the blank next to each description of an igneous rock and leave the space blank beside those descriptions that are not igneous rocks." <u>Eliciting Performance</u>

Teacher collects worksheets, corrects them and returns them to students on next day. Teacher also gives further explanation regarding items that several students missed. <u>Provide Feedback, Provide Learning Guidance</u>

A written test similar to the practice exercise just described will be given at the completion of the section of the Earth Science unit dealing with rock classifications. This test will measure students' ability to classify all three classifications of rocks (igneous, sedimentary and metamorphic). <u>Assessing Performance</u>

Igneous rocks will be reviewed as the class learns about sedimentary and metamorphic rock classifications. Students will also be asked to bring in sample rocks so that they can be identified by using a property chart. As the rocks are identified on the chart, students will also be asked to classify them by the way in which they were formed. <u>Enhancing Retention and Transfer</u>

(Note: Underlined events are considered to be the primary function(s) served by each lesson activity.)

NOTES

SELECTING AND USING MEDIA

Overview:

A great amount of energy has been spent on research to determine which medium is best for instruction. The inevitable conclusion is that it doesn't matter; all appear to be equally effective. Attention recently has turned from research on which medium is best to which attributes of a presentation are most important. Behind this line of thinking is the premise that many media share the same attributes, and that is what will determine which is effective and which is not. Gagné, Briggs and Wager take a slightly different view of media selection. Consistent with their theoretical position, they feel that the effectiveness of a medium will depend upon the instructional events and conditions of learning it can support. Therefore one has to look at the media selection process with regard to the type of learning involved and the events that are desired for a given learning population.

The major skill to be acquired in this chapter is the ability to select media which are appropriate for the types of learning, the types of learning situations, and the events of instruction. Use the verbal information and defined concept practice exercises to provide the background for you to apply the rules of selection correctly.

Objectives:

1. **When presented with an oral or written question, state:**

   a) the definition of instructional media.
   b) at least six factors affecting media selection decisions by listing and giving an example of each factor.
   c) six general types of learning situations that affect media selection decisions.
   d) what is meant by exclusionary factors in media selection. Give an example of three factors.
   e) what three practical factors most often affect media selection.
   f) what determines the level of abstraction of an educational experience according to Edgar Dale.

2. **Given descriptions of learning situations, classify** the six types of learning situations by recognizing examples of each type.

3. **Given lists of domains of learning outcomes, learning situations, and rules that pertain to the exclusion or selection of certain media or attributes, state** which rules go with each domain or learning situation by matching.

4. **Given a list of educational experiences, classify** their level of abstraction by placing them on Dale's Cone of Experience by level number.

5. **Given a variety of learning situations, demonstrate** the rules of exclusion and selection by indicating the most appropriate media for a specified learning situation.

Practice Exercises:

1. a) Define the term "instructional media."

    b) List and give an example of at least six of the eight general factors affecting media selection.

        (1)

        (2)

        (3)

        (4)

        (5)

        (6)

    c) List six general types of learning situations that affect media selection decisions.

        (1)   (4)

        (2)   (5)

        (3)   (6)

    d) What is meant by the term "exclusionary factors in media selection"?

        Give three examples of exclusionary factors:

        (1)

        (2)

        (3)

e) What three practical factors probably most influence a teacher's decision with regard to media selection?

(1)

(2)

(3)

2. Column A contains descriptions of learning situations. Column B contains the six types of learning situations. Match each description with its type by writing the letter corresponding to the type on the line to the left of each description. Each response in column B may be used once or more than once.

Column A	Column B
___1. Kindergarten children work on letter recognition at a learning center.	a. Central broadcast
b. High performance competence
___2. Instructor teaches principles of accounting to MBA students.	c. Instructor with non-readers
___3. Factory foreman teaches the operation of a drill press to a functionally illiterate employee.	d. Instructor with readers
e. Self-instruction with non-readers
___4. Corporate headquarters provides training for five regional plants simultaneously over a satellite network.	f. Self-instruction with readers
___5. Firefighters receive training in the operation of new equipment.
___6. ID students are assigned to read a chapter and complete practice exercises in a workbook.
___7. Medical students develop skills with surgical instruments.
___8. All buildings in a school district screen a PBS science program on Wednesdays at lO a.m.
___9. Lecturer uses printed case studies in an engineering class.
___10. Workshop participants complete a programmed text to review prior skills.

3A. Column A contains the types of learning situations. Column B contains exclusionary rules for media selection. Match the selection rule with its learning situation by writing the letter from column B on the line to the left of each situation in column A. Each response from column B may be used once, more than once, or not at all.

Column A

_____ 1. High performance competence

_____ 2. Central broadcast

_____ 3. Self-instruction with readers

_____ 4. Self-instruction with non-readers

_____ 5. Instructor with readers

_____ 6. Instructor with non-readers

Column B

a. All media are potentially effective

b. Exclude all media except large equipment, portable equipment, simulator

c. Exclude all media except radio and television broadcast

d. Exclude media using discursive printed passages or complex audio messages

e. Exclude interactive video simulation

f. Exclude printed texts and complex instructor lectures

g. Exclude training devices and training aids

3B. Column A contains the five general domains of learning. Column B contains exclusion rules. Match the rule with its domain by writing the letter corresponding to the rule on the line to the left of the domain. Each response may be used once or more than once. Some domains may require more than one response.

Column A

___1. Attitudes

___2. Cognitive Strategies

___3. Intellectual Skills

___4. Motor Skills

___5. Verbal Information

Column B

a. Exclude media with no provision for learner response and feedback.

b. Exclude media with no interactive feature.

c. Exclude only real equipment or simulator with no verbal accompaniments.

d. Exclude printed discourse for non-readers.

3C. Column A contains the five general domains of learning. Column B contains selection rules. Match the rule with its domain by writing the letter corresponding to the rule on the line to the left of the domain. Each response may be used once or more than once. Some domains may require more than one response.

Column A

___1. Attitudes

___2. Cognitive Strategies

___3. Intellectual Skills

___4. Motor Skills

___5. Verbal Information

Column B

a. Select audio and visual features for non-readers.

b. Select media able to present realistic pictures of human model and the model's message.

c. Select media able to present verbal messages and elaborations.

d. Select media making possible direct practice of the skill with informative feedback.

e. Select media providing feedback to learner responses.

4. The following diagram represents Dale's Cone of Experience. For each of the activities listed, write the number of the level of abstraction it represents by putting the number in the blank to the left of the activity.

___a) The kindergarten students visited Ashton's Farm.

___b) Money skills are enhanced by setting up a store in the classroom.

___c) The 10-year-olds watched a movie on pyramids.

___d) A group of mechanics watched a videotape on water pumps.

___e) The civics class listened to a speech by John F. Kennedy.

___f) The volleyball coach shows the difference between a spike and a bump.

___g) A teacher states orally the definition of "conservation".

___h) Home economics students prepare a three-course meal.

___i) Archeology students found the Rameses display very informative.

___j) Coast Guard recruits study a model of an icebreaker.

___k) A slide series illustrates cell biology.

___l) A map drawn on the chalkboard illustrated plotting coordinates.

___m) A piano teacher shows her pupil how to form a chord.

___n) A re-enactment by the class of the first Thanksgiving.

___o) Dissecting a frog.

___p) A small group discussion on types of learning.

___q) A tour of a television station by communications students.

___r) Children recreate the story of "Cinderella" using puppets.

___s) Geometric shapes were discussed on the overhead projector.

___t) Art students studied examples of Rembrandt on the opaque projector.

5. For each of the following learning situations designate the appropriate media. You may wish to list several alternatives that meet the selection rules. (HINT: First, specify the domain of learning and the learning situation. Then apply the selection and exclusion rules.)

   a) Kindergarten children work on letter recognition independently at a learning center.

   b) A factory foreman trains a functionally illiterate employee in the operation of a drill press.

   c) A lecturer is teaching accounting principles to MBA students.

   d) ID students learn about types of learning.

   e) Medical students learn to use surgical instruments.

   f) Teach a group of sixth-graders the major events of the Civil War.

   g) Teach problem-solving strategies to engineering students.

   h) Students in preschool appreciate the importance of cleanliness.

i)   A poor reader needs to learn the elements of the Constitution.

j)   Electronics students learn to recognize switch types.

Application Exercises:

1. Locate a text for a course with which you are familiar. Turn to any page or section and list the learning outcomes. List at least one alternative medium suitable for teaching these outcomes. Consider a variety of learning situations.

2. Describe a lecture given by one of your instructors, and discuss how it could have been improved by using media. Be specific.

Feedback for Practice Exercises:

1.   a) Instructional media are the physical means by which an instructional message is communicated.

        b) Learning situation, physical factors, learning task, learner variables, learning environment, economy, culture, and practical factors.

        c) High performance competence required, central broadcast, self-instruction with readers, self-instruction with non-readers, instructor with readers, and instructor with non-readers.

        d) Exclusionary factors are factors that cause one to reject a potentially effective medium. Examples might be economic, cultural, learning environment, learner, or practical factors.

        e) The most common practical factors are availability, feasibility, cost. Other practical factors are listed in the text e.g., group size, teacher capability, room.

        f) The level of abstraction is determined by how many features of reality the experience contains. Lower-level experiences are hands-on and participative, higher-level experiences are mediated and generally involve symbols that must be decoded for effective communication.

2.   1) e   6) f
        2) d   7) b
        3) c   8) a
        4) a   9) d
        5) b   10) f

3A.   1) b   4) d
        2) c   5) a
        3) a   6) f

3B.
1) c, d
2) b, d
3) b, d
4) a
5) c, d

3C.
1) b
2) e, a
3) d
4) d
5) c, a

4.
a) 5	f) 4	k) 9	p) 12
b) 2	g) 12	l) 11	q) 5
c) 8	h) 1	m) 4	r) 3
d) 7	i) 6	n) 3	s) 11
e) 10	j) 2	o) 1	t) 9

5.

	Type of Learning	Learning Situation	Rule(s)	Media
a)	IS	SI-NR	Exclude prose Feedback Audio/Visual	Computer with audio Interactive TV Slide-Tape Filmstrip
b)	MS	I-NR HPC	Exclude text & complex lectures Practice/feedback Equipment	Motion picture Television Slide-Tape Overhead Projector Chart Drill press
c)	IS	I-R	All media with feedback or interaction	Any media with which the instructor can give feedback e.g., text computer overhead projector chart
d)	IS	I-R SI-R	Same as (c) Same as (c)	Same as (c) Same as (c)
e)	MS	HPC	Equipment Practice/feedback	Surgical instruments & cadaver/model

f)	VI	I-R	Verbal message & elaborations Exclude real equipment	All media are potentially effective except equipment e.g., video, text, chart
g)	CS	I-R	Same as (c)	Same as (c)
h)	A	I-NR	Realistic model No prose	Television Film Slide/tape
i)	VI	I-NR SI-NR	No prose Audio/visual Exclude real equipment No complex lecture	Video Film Slide/tape Filmstrip Chart Overhead projector
j)	IS	I-R	Same as (c)	Same as (c)
		SI-R	Same as (c)	Same as (c)

Criteria for Evaluating the Application Exercises:

1. Is the content correctly categorized by type of learning?

2. Have the exclusionary rules been applied for that type of learning?

3. Have the selection rules been applied for that type of learning?

4. Have the exclusionary rules been applied for the learning situation specified?

5. Do the media selected reflect the appropriate features required?

Examples of the Application Exercise:

EXAMPLE 1.A. Textbook Content (Gagné, Briggs, and Wager - Chapter 3)

Content: Five categories of learning outcomes

Types of learning: Defined concepts (IS) and verbal information. (Refer to the objectives listed at the beginning of Chapter 3 in this guide.)

Learning Situation	Media
a) Self-instruction with readers	Any media providing feedback Text/worksheets Computer
b) Instructor with readers	Any media providing feedback Text/handout Overhead Projector Chart

EXAMPLE 1.B. Textbook content (Elementary Science)

Content: Using a thermometer

Type of learning: Intellectual Skill (procedure)

Learning Situation	Media
a) Self-instruction with readers	Any media allowing for practice and feedback Thermometer Computer Movie Video Chart/text Filmstrip/slide/audiotape
b) Self-instruction with non-readers	same as (a) Exclude text
c) Instructor with readers	same as (a) Overhead projector
d) Instructor with non-readers	same as (a) and (c) Exclude text

EXAMPLE 2.   This is a description of a lecture from an educational psychology course. The instructor was lecturing about three different theories of learning; 1) developmental, 2)behavioristic, and 3) cognitive. The learning outcomes were mostly verbal information, with possibly some defined concept learning. The presentation style used was typical classroom lecture. The teacher used the blackboard, putting up key words

and names. The students in the class wrote notes furiously as the teacher talked.

The teacher could have improved the lecture by using an overhead projector with accompanying hand-outs and practice questions. This would have provided a context for notes, and would have provided practice, and given feedback over the information and concepts. He could even have used a film, if one was available, showing an advocate of each of the three theories. A film with human models might have made the theories more memorable by affecting attitudes towards the theories. Finally, the teacher could have given an assignment where groups of students designed a 10-minute role play situation for one of the three theories. The groups could have presented their role play for the class, reinforcing the concepts associated with each theory.

NOTES

DESIGNING THE INDIVIDUAL LESSON

Overview:

Lesson planning combines two activities: (1) planning course, unit, or topic sequences, and (2) incorporating the events of instruction into the lesson. Chapter 12 uses a four-step approach to lesson planning. These steps include listing the objectives, listing desired instructional events, choosing materials and activities, and noting roles for teachers and designers. A variety of information and practice activities is provided in this chapter to help you design individual lessons. One of the most useful is the lesson planning sheet which shows the relationships of activities to the events of instruction, taking into account the available instructional time.

Objectives:

1. **When presented with an oral or written question, state:**

   a) in your own words, definitions of the following:
      (1) mastery learning
      (2) adaptive instruction
      (3) "open-media" model of instruction

   b) a rule of thumb for using a learning hierarchy to establish a sequence for intellectual skill learning

   c) the repercussions of allowing learners to choose the sequence of instruction for intellectual skills

   d) what is meant by "teaching new cognitive strategies" and give an example of a strategy that might be taught

   e) the most important prerequisite for learning of verbal information

   f) four strategies for encoding names or labels

   g) contrasting methods for encoding facts and organized information

   h) the capabilities which constitute prerequisite skills for learning motor skills

   i) the purpose for incorporating the events of instruction in individual lessons

   j) the biggest difference(s) in applying the events of instruction to teacher-led versus mediated instruction

2. **Presented with a written question listing instructional activities, generate** a simple sequence for designing a lesson by ordering the activities in writing.

3. **Given a list of learning conditions, classify** the correct learning outcome for a specific instructional event by writing that outcome for the following events:

a) Event 3: stimulating recall of prior learning
b) Event 4: presenting the stimulus
c) Event 5: providing learner guidance
d) Event 6: eliciting performance

4. **Using an instructional curriculum map which you have constructed, generate** a time sequence of instructional activities which shows the relationship of instructional activities to instructional events by writing them in the format shown on page 125 of this guide.

5. **Using an instructional curriculum map which you have constructed, generate** a lesson planning sheet which indicates teaching activity, possible media, prescriptions for learning, and rationales for the reasoning behind the prescriptions by writing them in the format shown on pages 126-127 of this guide.

Practice Exercises:

1. a) (1) What is mastery learning?

(2) To what does the term "adaptive instruction" usually refer?

(3) What is the "open-media" model of instruction?

b) How can a learning hierarchy be used to establish a rough sequence for intellectual skill learning?

c) When is it less preferable to let learners choose the sequence of learning with intellectual skills?

d) What is meant by "teaching new cognitive strategies" to learners? Also, give an example that might be taught.

e) What is the most important prerequisite for the learning of verbal information?

f) Describe four strategies for encoding names or labels.

(1)

(2)

(3)

(4)

g) Contrast the procedures for sequencing information for individual facts versus organized information.

h) Describe the capabilities which constitute prerequisite skills for motor skill learning.

i) What is the purpose for incorporating the events of instruction in individual lessons?

j) What is the biggest difference in applying the events of instruction to teacher-led versus mediated instruction?

2. Indicate a sequence for designing a lesson by writing 1, 2, 3, and 4 in the blanks next to the actions below.

_____ classify lesson objectives

_____ implement the instructional prescription by writing the lesson content

_____ arrange specific events in an appropriate sequence to attain lesson objectives

_____ assure that the events of instruction are provided for

3. Separate learning conditions are listed under particular events of instruction below. Next to each of these, choose which of the following types of lesson objectives is most appropriate and indicate your choice in the space provided: (d) discrimination; (cc) concrete concept; (dc) defined concept; (r) rule; (ps) problem solving; (cs) cognitive strategy; (n) names or labels; (f) facts; (k) knowledge; (a) attitude; (ms) motor skill.

a) Event 3: stimulating recall of prior learning

_____ In learning to figure a course to avoid on a Navy ship, John must first recall relevant subordinate rules.

_____ The president must practice recall of associations to greet each member of congress by his or her first name.

_____ Years of training and study are required as well as recall of discrimination of relevant features for an art expert to tell that some "masterpieces" are fakes.

_____ A great running back succeeds in football partially because of recall of responses and part skills.

_____ Sherlock Holmes was a master at recalling related meaningful information in the appropriate context.

b) Event 4: presenting the stimulus

_____ In learning geometric shapes, presentation of several instances and noninstances varying in physically irrelevant object qualities is required.

_____ To promote the learning of related behavioral psychology tenets, the professor presented several instances and noninstances varying in irrelevant attributes.

_____ To learn the difference between fabrics, the intern was presented with same and different stimuli, with emphasis on distinctive features.

_____ In presenting a new wrestling maneuver, the coach arranged a situation requiring skill performance and use of executive subroutines.

_____ Accustomed to "real doozies" from their physics instructor, the students are not surprised by the presentation of a novel learning task or problem.

c) Event 5: providing learner guidance

_____ The swimming coach used a special harness and verbal input to assist with the establishment of an executive subroutine (procedural rule).

_____ In teaching the newcomer ways to "beat the system," the sly old fox used verbal statements or demonstrations of strategy.

_____ To encourage positive behavior, young detainees are rewarded for personal action, either by direct experience or vicariously by observation of human role models.

_____ The camp counselors walk through a demonstration of camp procedures using verbal statements.

_____ To help her students learn history information, the teacher presents the information in an elaborated context.

d) Event 6: eliciting performance

_____ The children were asked to identify physical instances of many types of trucks on today's highways.

_____ To be sure that the young tribesman could tell the difference between the desired rope and an inferior brand, repetition of the same and different ropes with feedback was required.

_____ Some history essay questions require the performance of reinstating new knowledge in the context of related information.

_____ Nothing less than practice of the total skill is suitable to learn to perform the "Eskimo roll" before actually attacking the white water.

_____ Susan showed that she had acquired the procedural background necessary in copying a computer file by demonstration of a rule example.

Application Exercise:

1. For the objectives in a lesson-level instructional curriculum map (such as the one you may have completed for Chapter 8 of this workbook) prepare an objectives by events time-line, again using the lesson objectives from assignment 4. Group the events into reasonable learning activities, and specify the media and stimuli for each activity on your lesson planning sheet (see component 2 of this assignment). For examples, see page 236 in Gagné, Briggs, and Wager text. Also, see student example at the end of this chapter.

2. Prepare a lesson planning sheet (referenced to your objectives by events time-line). The lesson planning sheet should include media selection, prescription, and a rationale for each learning activity. Your rationale for the lesson strategy should be based on the target audience, and the learning environment. Again, see the student example at the end of this chapter.

Feedback for Practice Exercises:

1. a) (1) Using mastery learning, achievement rather than time is the criterion for a student's progress through instruction.

   (2) Adaptive instruction consists of materials which use a management system which constantly monitors a students progress through a module. Instructional content is then prescribed based on a student's on-task performance.

   (3) In the "open-media" model of instructional design, prescriptions are written before media are chosen, allowing designers a wider latitude with which they can make decisions.

   b) As a general rule of thumb, a lower-level skill in a learning hierarchy should be taught before a skill defined in the level above.

c) A basic premise of intellectual skill learning is that students should master an essential prerequisite skill before proceeding on to an upper-level skill. Mastery implies that learners achieve confidence in performing a skill to a degree of completeness required for later attainment of an upper-level skill. Because learners are less likely to be aware of requirements for unlearned upper-level skills, the sequence of instruction for prerequisite skills should be prescribed by the instructor or instructional designer. In instances where two or more skills occupy the same level of a learning hierarchy, however, allowing the learner to choose may be a perfectly acceptable strategy.

d) "Teaching a new cognitive strategy" suggests that the student is introduced to a new way of processing information. For example, using the peg word system to memorize procedural lists is more effective than not using a system in the beginning stages of learning.

e) Providing a meaningful context with which newly learned information can be subsumed or associated in a meaningful sense is the most important prerequisite for learning verbal information.

f) Four strategies for encoding names or labels are summarized below.

  (1) Simple associations often involve associating a newly encountered name or label with one more familiar to the learner.

  (2) Names or labels could be encoded by making the letters or parts of the word into a sentence which is easy to recall.

  (3) Associating a name with a concrete visual image representing that name is frequently used by those adept at remembering people's names.

  (4) Another mnemonic technique involves the use of lists of keywords which "peg" names or labels to unusual concrete images, thus making it easier to recall arbitrarily organized information.

g) One procedure for learning factual information involves the prior learning (in a sequence) of "organizers" which inform the learner of major distinctive categories and then follows with specific facts. A second procedure uses questions or statements to identify major categories of facts, assuming that prior learning of facts in a larger context will facilitate the learning of them. In sequencing organized information, one should take into account existing schemas which may be used by the learner to subsume existing information.

h) Part skills (which compose "segments" of the skill to be learned) and an executive subroutine (the complex rule controls the execution of the part skills) are the two major capabilities which constitute prerequisite skills for motor learning.

i) The events of instruction are incorporated into a lesson to arrange the external conditions of learning in such a way that learning (the internal conditions) occurs.

j) A teacher can fill in the gaps in the events of instruction whereas mediated instruction requires the designer to consider all the events.

2. The most logical sequence would probably be 1, 4, 3, and 2.

3. Effective learning conditions for specific types of lesson objectives are indicated below.

   a) Event 3: stimulating recall of prior learning

   problem solving ...   recall of relevant subordinate rules

   name or label ...   recall of associations

   concrete concept...   recall of discrimination of relevant features

   motor skill ...   recall of responses and part skills

   fact ...   recall of context of related meaningful information

   b) Event 4: presenting the stimulus

   concrete concept...   presentation of several instances and noninstances varying in physically irrelevant object qualities

   defined concept ...   presentation of several instances and noninstances varying in irrelevant attributes

   discrimination...   presentation of same and different stimuli, with emphasis on distinctive features

   motor skill...   presentation of a situation requiring skill performance and use of executive subroutines

   problem solving...   presentation of a novel learning task or problem

   c) Event 5: providing learner guidance

   motor skill...   establishment of executive subroutine (procedural rule)

   cognitive strategy...   verbal statement or demonstration of strategy

   attitude...   reward for personal action, either by direct experience or vicariously by observation of the human model

   rule...   demonstration of rule using verbal statement

   fact...   using fact in context of other knowledge

   d) Event 6: eliciting performance

   concrete concept ..   identification of physical instances by student

   discrimination ....   repetition of same and different stimuli, with feedback

knowledge...	performance of reinstating new knowledge in the context of related information
motor skill...	practice of total skill
rule...	demonstration of rule example by student

Criteria for Evaluating the Application Exercise:

1. Are all the objectives represented on the time-line?

2. Are the events selected sufficient for the objectives and target audience?

3. Are the stimuli and learning activities congruent, can they be delivered by the chosen medium in the allotted time?

4. Are the instructional activities well sequenced, and reasons given for omissions or consolidation of events?

5. Are the media reasonable for the target audience and the learning environment? (10%)

6. Do the prescriptions describe the learning activities in enough detail so that they may be easily scripted?

An example of an objectives by events time-line from a student project by Dave Proulx

```
EDM 593: Practicum in Instructional Design
Assignment 6: Time/Activity Instructional Sequence
Dave Proulx
```

Course Title: Fundamentals of Office Automation

		(a)	(b)	(c)	(d)	(e)
O B J E C T I V E S	3.2.1.1: Given a list of customer profiles, each student will state definitions of each customer profile by writing.	1-2	4-5	6-7		
	3.2.1.2: Given a list of desired reports, each student will demonstrate selecting the appropriate customer profile by writing the profile type next to each report description.		3-4-5	6-7		
	3.2.1: Given the Datawaste computer, the company's customer database system, and a specification sheet, each student will demonstrate printing a customer phone roster by printing a roster.				3-4-5	6-7
	3.2.2: Given the Datawaste computer, the company's customer database system, and a specification sheet, each student will demonstrate printing a customer mailing list by printing a list.				3-4-5	6-7
	3.2.3: Given the Datawaste computer, the company's customer database system, and a specification sheet, each student will demonstrate printing a monthly or annual sales report by printing reports.				3-4-5	6-7
E N T R Y S K I L L S	Unit 1: Given the Datawaste computer, each student will execute proper use of the system hardware by powering on the system, loading, booting, and removing a floppy disk, and powering off the system.				9	
	Lesson 3.1: Given the Datawaste computer, the company's customer database system, and sample customer data, each student will demonstrate database maintenance by adding, editing, backing up, and restoring the data.		9		9	
	Intro to data systems: Each student will summarize the contents of database reports by writing a description of each type of report.				9	
	Instructional Activities	(a)	(b)	(c)	(d)	(e)

Minutes: 0   5   20   30   40   50

An example of a lesson planning sheet from a student project by David Proulx

Course Title: Fundamentals of Office Automation

		Media	Prescription	Rationale
L E A R N I N G A C T I V I T I E S	(a)	Text, Overhead projector	Gain attention: Ask students, "Who buys our products?" Discuss the concept of analyzing customers according to different categories. Inform students of objectives: "In this lesson you'll learn several ways of grouping customers, then you'll learn how to run database reports using those groups."	Provide printed copies of objectives 3.2.1.1, 3.2.1.2, 3.2.1, 3.2.2, and 3.2.3. Target audience consists of literate office workers. Environment will support text handouts and overhead projectors.
	(b)	Text, Overhead projector	Recall Prerequisites: Review types of customer information stored in the database. Remind students that the pieces of information are stored separately and may be reorganized in almost any order. Present material: Define term "Customer profile": A way of grouping customers so that they can be studied in useful ways". List profiles available in the company database (By zip code, by area code, by sales amount, and by age.) Have students think of examples where each profile might be used. Provide guidance: Insure that students understand when to select each profile from the database.	Provide printed copies of database record descriptions. Target audience consists of literate office workers. Environment will support text handouts and overhead projectors.

An example of a lesson planning sheet from a student project by David Proulx (continued)

		Media	Prescription	Rationale
L E A R N I N G A C T I V I T I E S	(c)	Text, Overhead projector	<u>Elicit performance</u>: Give examples of company reports and ask students to select a profile that would best fit the report. (Example: ˙The company is going to have a sale at our Mobile store. Which profile would you use to mail a flyer to all our customers in the Mobile area?˙) <u>Provide feedback</u>: Give students correct answers and explain why the choices are correct.	Provide printed copies of sample report requests. Target audience consists of literate office workers. Environment will support text handouts and overhead projectors.
	(d)	Training device	<u>Recall Prerequisites</u>: Give each student a floppy disk containing the sample database they created in Lesson 3.1. Have students boot their computers and Load the sample database into the database program. Review the three reports available from the company database. Have students set up printers. <u>Present material</u>: Walk students through the process of selecting a customer profile, picking a report type, then giving any parameters (month, zip codes, area codes, etc.) required to run the report. <u>Provide guidance</u>: Give sample situations and help students select the best profile and report for each case.	Provide Datawaste computer and floppy disk containing sample data. Target audience consists of literate office workers. Environment will support training devices (one computer and one floppy per student) and text.
	(e)	Training device, Text	<u>Elicit performance</u>: Give examples of situations that call for students to select a profile and report to accomplish the desired result. <u>Provide feedback</u>: Give students correct answers and explain why the choices are correct.	Provide Datawaste computer and floppy disk containing sample data. Target audience consists of literate office workers. Environment will support training devices (one computer and one floppy disk per student) and text.

NOTES

ASSESSING STUDENT PERFORMANCE

Overview:

This chapter focuses attention on measuring what the student knows about the stated curriculum objectives. We use the term objective-referenced assessment because the object is to measure the students' mastery of the skills, not how well they score in relation to other students in the group. Grades are seen as a way of indicating mastery, so it is conceivable that all the students could get A's or they could all get F's, depending on how well they performed the skills. The chapter discusses evaluation concepts, and criteria for measuring different types of learning outcomes.

Objectives:

1. When presented with an oral or written question, state:

    a) Four different purposes served by assessment.

    b) definitions of the following terms:
        validity
        mastery
        reliability

    c) important criteria in the evaluation of:
        verbal information
        concepts
        rules
        attitudes
        motor skills

    d) the differences between criterion and norm referenced assessment.

2. Given an objective, and a test item over that objective, classify the test items as valid or invalid for the objective. Given a performance objective, generate test items that are valid for that objective.

3. Given a set of objectives for a lesson you have written, generate a valid and reliable test for that lesson.

Practice Exercises:

1. a) List and briefly describe four different purposes served by assessment.

    (1)

    (2)

    (3)

    (4)

b) Define each of the following terms:

validity

mastery

reliability

c) List at least one important criterion in the evaluation of each of the following:

verbal information

concepts

rules

problem solving

attitudes

motor skills

d) Describe the major difference between criterion and norm referenced assessment.

2. For each of the following objectives determine if the test item that follows is valid, and if not rewrite it so that it would be valid.

a) objective: Given a piece of animal tissue, the student will demonstrate dehydration of that specimen using the alcohol method.

a) test item: Explain how you would dehydrate a piece of rat muscle tissue using the alcohol dehydration procedure.

_____This item is VALID, NOT VALID (if not valid, then rewrite it so that it is).

b) objective: Given a labeled tissue specimen the student will generate an adequate stained slide by determining an appropriate fixation and staining technique.

b) test item: In the refrigerator is a labeled tissue specimen. Prepare a properly fixated and stained slide including a brief description of the technique you used to prepare the slide.

_____This item is VALID, NOT VALID (if not valid, then rewrite it so that it is).

c) objective: Given a list of solutions, classify those that are vaso-dialators.

c) test item: Look at the attached list of medical solutions, circle those that are vaso-dialators.

_____This item is VALID, NOT VALID (if not valid, then rewrite it so that it is).

d) objective: The students will choose to read and apply educational research in their teaching.

d) test item: Describe three findings from educational research that have implications for teaching.

_____This item is VALID, NOT VALID (if not valid, then rewrite it so that it is).

e) objective: Student will be able to identify specific human musculature by attaching electrodes to appropriate sites.

e) test item: Place an electrode on your lab partner at each of the following muscle sites: upper deltoid, triceps, biceps, ham string, pectoral. Call the teacher when you have finished and are ready to be checked out.

_____This item is VALID, NOT VALID (if not valid, then rewrite it so that it is).

f) objective: Given an EKG, the student classifies areas of electrical activity by circling them on the graph.

f) test item: Using the copy of the EKG attached to your paper, circle the areas that represent muscle contractions.

_____This item is VALID, NOT VALID (if not valid, then rewrite it so that it is).

g) objective: Given a list of psychological components of response time, the student adopts a method of imagery to verbalize all components.

g) test item: Prior to the end of lab class, discuss with the instructor the components of response time, and explain what method of memorization you used to remember this information.

_____This item is VALID, NOT VALID (if not valid, then rewrite it so that it is).

h) objective: State the functions of dendrites and axons within a neuron.

h) test item: Neurons are composed of dendrites and axons, what are their functions?

_____This item is VALID, NOT VALID (if not valid, then rewrite it so that it is).

i) objective: Given a model of typeset text separated by 1-em spaces and 2-em spaces, the student will be able to discriminate a 1-em space from a 2-em space.

i) test item: Look at the attached typeset manuscript. Using the spacing model provided as a guide, mark the manuscript with a check-mark where you <u>do not</u> find a 1-em space between words and a 2-em space between sentences.

_____This item is VALID, NOT VALID (if not valid, then rewrite it so that it is).

j) objective: Given 10 photographs, five each of two different levels of sharpness and grain, the student will discriminate the levels of sharpness by sorting the photographs with like sharpness into two piles.

j) test item: On the front desk is a pile of 10 photographs, five have one level of sharpness and grain and five have a different level. Sort them into two piles, putting those with like sharpness together.

_____This item is VALID, NOT VALID (if not valid, then rewrite it so that it is).

k) objective: Given several types of plastic materials, the student will be able to identify those that are suitable for use on the overhead projector.

k) test item: Look at the 10 samples of plastic visuals labeled A-Z. Tell how you would determine if they are suitable for overhead projection.

_____This item is VALID, NOT VALID (if not valid, then rewrite it so that it is).

l) objective: Given several visual illustrations, the student will be able to classify them as balanced or unbalanced.

l) test item: Determine if each of the first 10 visual illustrations in your text is balanced or unbalanced by writing balanced or unbalanced alongside the number of each illustration.

_____This item is VALID, NOT VALID (if not valid, then rewrite it so that it is).

m) objective: Given a presentation topic, e.g., the Western movement, the student will generate a visual that illustrates that topic.

m) test item: Create an illustration that would help you to teach the water cycle. The illustration must be well balanced, correctly labeled, and show effective use of color.

_____This item is VALID, NOT VALID (if not valid, then rewrite it so that it is).

n) objective: Given a set of data, the student will demonstrate the construction of a line graph to represent the data.

n) test item: Construct a line graph based on the following cost of mailing a first class letter. 1952, .03; 1958, .04; 1963, .05; 1968, .06; 1971, .08; 1974, .10; 1975, .13; 1978, .15; 1981, .20.

_____This item is VALID, NOT VALID (if not valid, then rewrite it so that it is).

o) objective: The student will be able to state the characteristics of a good graph.

o) test item: Describe why it is important to create a good graph.

_____This item is VALID, NOT VALID (if not valid, then rewrite it so that it is).

Application Exercises:

Write a post-test for a unit or lesson you plan to teach. Explain how you would grade this test. Have a friend match each objective to one or more of the test items. Does their analysis agree with yours? If not, why not?

Create a diagnostic test for the same unit or lesson. How does it differ from the mastery post-test?

Feedback for Practice Exercises:

1. a) List and briefly describe four different purposes served by assessment:
    (1) Diagnosis of student difficulties. To determine what prerequisite skills are creating problems in learning new material.

    (2) Placement within an instructional program. To place the student in an appropriate level of study.

    (3) Checking student progress. To aid in the management of the student's time.

    (4) Reporting to school and parents. A way of indicating which skills the student has mastered compared to what is expected.

    b) Define each of the following terms:

    validity: The degree to which the test item represents the behavior specified in the objective.

    mastery: A level of performance of a skill that indicates that the skill has been learned.

    reliability: The degree of stability of a measure of a learner's skill. The higher the reliability, the greater one's confidence that the assessment has yielded an accurate estimate rather than chance performance.

    c) List at least one important criterion in the evaluation of each of the following:

    verbal information   recall of the information stated in the objective (as opposed to recognition of the information).

    concepts   Classification of instances or noninstances of the concept as opposed to simply recognizing or recalling a definition.

    rules   Give the learners an appropriate situation and ask them to apply the rule.

    problem solving   In the response the student should show synthesis of applicable rules.

    attitudes   Attitudes should almost always be observed unobtrusively.

    motor skills   The test should require performance of the motor skill being assessed. Description of the skill is not an adequate test.

d) Describe the major difference between criterion and normative referenced assessment. Criterion referenced assessment uses a pre-stated standard for acceptable performance. A normative assessment uses a standard derived from the average performance of the group being assessed.

2. a) This item is NOT VALID because it calls for verbal information performance; the test item calls for rule using. A better item would be: Go to the refrigerator and get a specimen from the package labeled "animal tissue." Dehydrate the tissue using the alcohol method. Have the teacher check your final product.

b) This item is VALID.

c) At first this item looks to be VALID because the observable performance matches the skill required by the objective. However, here the objective is suspect. How could one classify vaso-dialators from a list (unless the name contained one of the attributes of the defined concept?) This should be a verbal information objective, in which case the item would be valid. However, it would still not be a very good item since it involves recognition rather than recall.

d) This item is NOT VALID. To measure an attitude you would have to observe what the teacher does and make inferences regarding the choice behavior. The attitude could not be tested directly by asking the student to state something.

e) This item is VALID.

f) This item is NOT VALID. The objective calls for electrical activity; the test item calls for muscle contraction; if these two terms are synonymous, then the nomenclatue in the objective should include both to produce a valid test item.

g) This item is VALID. The criteria for judging a student's response should include recognition of the strategy that was adopted (assuming one was taught).

h) This item appears to be acceptable, but it is NOT VALID because it is poorly written and probably not reliable. Some of the students are going to think the question means what are the functions of the neurons, and others are going to think it wants the functions of the dendrites and axons. Rewrite to ask, "What are the functions of the dendrites and axons within a neuron?"

i) This item is VALID. A discrimination task only requires that the student can detect differences between two stimuli. A test item should contain a model to which the stimulus being discriminated can be compared.

j) This item is VALID.

k) This item is NOT VALID. The objective calls for concrete concept recognition of transparent material; the test item calls for verbal information regarding what works on an overhead. Better item -- select from the pile of 10 illustrations on plastic those that would be suitable for use on an overhead projector.

l) This item is VALID.

m) This item is VALID. However, if the quality of the visual is to be evaluated the criteria for evaluation should be included in the objective (under tools, constratints or special conditions.)

n) This item is VALID, but the item could be a little more complete.

o) This item is NOT VALID. The objective calls for information about the characteristics; the test item calls for information about reasons for quality graphs. The item should read, "What are the characteristics of a good graph?"

Criteria for Evaluating the Application Exercises:

1. Does the post-test contain items for each major objective in the unit or lesson?

2. Do the items accurately access the skill reflected by the objective? (Is the test valid?)

3. Are the number of items for each objective sufficient to have confidence that proficiency on the test would reflect reliable performance on the skills being measured? (Is the test reliable?)

4. Are the two tests (mastery test and diagnostic test) appropriate for the purposes to be served?

5. Is the grading system adequately described and defended?

The pages that follow contain an example of the application exercises done by a student, Edna Holland Mory. Only parts 1 and 2 of her total 4-part exercise are included because of space limitations.

```
Post-test:   Specification of Items to Objectives
             and Grading System
```

Part 1 test items assess performance on objective 5.1. Part 2 test items assess performance on objective 5.3. And Part 3 test items assess performance on objective 5.4, the terminal objective for this lesson.

Since the other objectives are either prerequisites from previous lessons or merely verbal information to aid in the performance of the skill, they are not specifically tested. It is assumed that if the student can successfully demonstrate the performance of the tested objectives, he possesses these prerequisite skills as well.

The number of post-test items should be enough to adequately assess whether or not the student has mastered the skills in the lesson. Since the demonstration of correct use of particular rules is measured through a repetition employing a variety of examples, it is not necessary to give a lengthy list, as long as the examples chosen cover the representative range of possible offerings. This would be done by giving examples that use both sharp and flat keys, that start on both black and white keys, that require use of writing in both treble and bass clefs, and that give varying numbers of sharps/flats in the key signatures. The items in the test reflect this.

Grading is based on a mastery of the use of the rule. 90% mastery or better would be given a grade of A, 80% a B, and 70% a C. Anything less than the 70% mastery would not be acceptable to continue on through the lessons. This approach would hold true at the end of the course as well, with at least a 70% mastery required as a very minimum performance.

Items will be marked off according to number of errors within each response. For example, writing out a scale will require many different skills such as starting on the correct note, writing the notes consecutively on the lines and spaces, and including the correct accidentals. The amount counted off for each of these depends on whether the error was for a minor skill, such as leaving out a single accidental, or for writing a scale that is totally wrong.

In addition, assessment of certain prerequisite skills can be
seen by the varying performances required on the test. A good
example of this can be seen in **Part 2**, when the student is not
allowed to use a key signature at all. These items will show up
misunderstandings in the specific whole step/half step pattern of
the scale, along with correct usage of the accidentals themselves.

The items in **Part 3** compose 50% of the test, since these items
cover the terminal objective of this particular lesson. Items in
Part 1 and **Part 2** are targeting the subordinate skills toward the
learning of the terminal objective. They are not weighted as high,
but there is still the need to access them separately to uncover
any specific areas of inadequacies.

Lesson Level ICM for
Lesson 5
by Edna Holland Mory

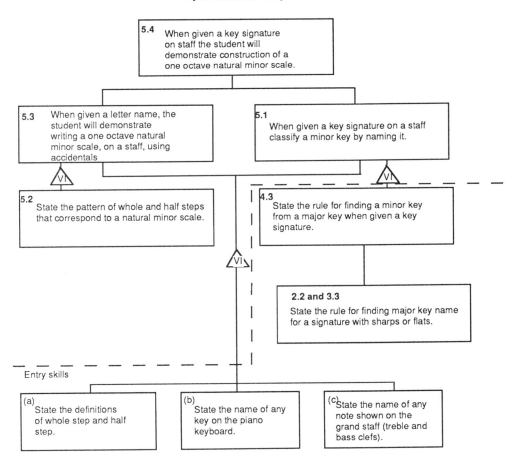

Post-test for Lesson 5

Part 1.   Write the name of the minor key for each of the following key
signatures.

1. _____ Minor

2. _____ Minor

3. _____ Minor

4. _____ Minor

5. _____ Minor

Part 2. Write a one-octave ascending and descending natural minor scale from the given starting note. Use only accidentals instead of a key signature.

Diagnostic Test: Specification of Items to Objectives

Part 1 test items cover objectives: 1.2
                                        7.2

Part 2 test items cover objectives: 1.3
                                        5.3
                                        6.2
                                        6.4

Part 3 test items cover objectives: 2.3
                                        3.3
                                        4.1
                                        5.1

Part 4 test items cover objectives: 4.2
                                        5.4
                                        7.3
                                        7.4

Any remaining objectives require merely to state verbal information used as specific prerequisite knowledge to the learning of the objectives listed above. It is assumed that if the students can successfully demonstrate adequate performance on the tested objectives, then they would have these prerequisite skills as well, but not necessarily vice versa.

The Diagnostic Test includes at least one item for each type of scale covered in the lesson -- major, natural minor, harmonic minor, melodic minor. Items range from being able to recognize the scale when it is already given, recognizing key signatures for both major and minor keys, writing a scale when given a key signature, and writing a scale when given its name.

Diagnostic (Placement) Test

Part 1.   Write the name of each of the following scales, and tell whether it
          is major, natural minor, harmonic minor, or melodic minor.

1. ____

2. ____

3. ____

4. ____

5. ____

Part 2. Write a one-octave ascending and descending scale in each of the following keys, according to type of scale specified.

(1) B^b Harmonic Minor

(2) F Major

(3) G$^\#$ Natural Minor

(4) C$^\#$ Major

(5) E Melodic Minor

GROUP INSTRUCTION

Overview:

The characteristics of group instruction are examined in Chapter 14 through an analysis of the efficiency and effectiveness with which the events of instruction can be delivered in two-person group (tutoring), small group and large group instructional arrangements. Some of the events are more problematic than others, but all are affected by the nature of instructional interactions in groups of various sizes. As the size of the group increases, the degree of certainty of instructional control over achievement of the various events diminishes. Also, self-instructional strategies become increasingly important in determining learning outcomes.

There is discussion of the distinguishing patterns of interaction between instructor and learners in groups of various sizes. Also examined are recitation, discussion groups and the lecture. Strategies to overcome the inherent limitations of small and particularly large group instruction are suggested, including mastery learning and enhancement of prerequisites, cues, and learner participation.

The learner should give careful attention to the ways that events of instruction are delivered and to the probable effectiveness of instructional events as the size of a group increases. Exercises for this chapter emphasize knowledge of the instructional characteristics and consequences of different sized groups. They are also intended to engage the learner in a review of the implications for adaptations to group size that can improve the effectiveness of the events of instruction for individual students despite wide variations in group size.

Objectives:

1. When asked, in the form of an oral or written question, state:

    a)   three (3) basic types of instructional groups and the forms of instruction that are most often associated with each

    b)   the patterns of interaction that accompany tutoring, recitation and the lecture

    c)   why tutoring is such an effective means of instruction and what factors ultimately determine whether or not it is successful

    d)   how the control of instructional events varies in a two-person group, a small group, and in large group instruction and the reasons for this

    e)   how small group instruction facilitates the diagnosis of students' prior learning

    f)   why instruction in discussion groups may be characterized as "interactive communication"

    g)   the two types of learning outcomes for which the group discussion form is particularly well suited

    h)   the characteristics of problems that stimulate learners to engage in meaningful problem-solving behavior

i) how the events of instruction can be achieved with the lecture

j) the names of four (4) events of instruction that can be achieved through questions in recitation

k) why there is such limited precision in controlling events of instruction in large group recitation classes

l) the procedural features of a mastery learning system and reasons for the success of this approach

m) the relationships among achievement in large group instruction, mastery learning and tutoring according to the text

n) ways to enhance the effectiveness of large group instruction so that it may approximate the results of tutoring

Practice Exercises:

1.   a)   What are the three (3) basic types of instructional groups and what learning activities are typically associated with each?

          (1)

          (2)

          (3)

        b)   What are the typical patterns of interaction (communication) associated with:

          (1) Tutoring

          (2) Recitation in small or large groups

          (3) The lecture method

        c)   Why is tutoring such an effective means of instruction? What actually determines whether tutoring will be successful?

d) Is the control of instructional events in small group instruction more similar to control in two-person groups or large groups? Why?

e) In what ways does small group instruction facilitate diagnosis of students' prior learning?

f) Why is instruction in discussion groups characterized as "interactive communication"?

g) In addition to general subject matter mastery, what categories of learning outcomes are most often sought through discussion group tasks?

h) According to Maier, what are the characteristics of problems that facilitate problem solving through group discussion?

i) Can the events of instruction be effectively achieved with the lecture? Explain.

j)   Name four of the events of instruction that can be achieved through questions in a recitation class.

k)   Why is control of instructional events so imprecise for large group recitation classes?

l)   Describe the typical procedure used in a mastery learning system. How does this approach enhance learning?

m)   In terms of achievement, how does large group instruction compare with mastery learning procedures and with tutoring?

n)   How can the effectiveness of tutoring be approximated in large group instruction?

Application Exercise:

Study the lesson plan in exercise 3A of Chapter 10 of this guide (page 95). Revise this lesson for small group instruction being careful to use what is known about the advantages of this grouping arrangement for achieving certain events of instruction.

Feedback for Practice Exercises:

1. a) The two-person group makes tutoring possible. The small group (3-8) lends itself to both discussion and interactive recitation, where group members give feedback regarding the performance of peers. With large groups (15 or more), the lecture is the most typical form and may be accompanied by projected media and demonstrations.

    b) In the two-person group, communication flows from teacher to student and vice versa. Recitation generally involves mutual interaction between teacher and one student and one-way communication with other students. Interactive recitation stimulates dialogue among students as well. In the typical lecture, communication flows from teacher to students.

    c) The two-person group provides instructors with great flexibility in adjusting instructional events to match learners' needs. Tutoring is successful when it ensures that instructional events are carefully and systematically controlled. (Review pages 271-272 for examples of adjustments to the events of instruction that are possible with tutoring.)

    d) Small group instruction approximates the conditions found in tutoring. Instructional events can be more effectively tailored (using tutorial methods) to the individual learners in small groups since students take turns responding and teachers can also simultaneously direct instruction to more than one learner.

    e) Questioning of each student is more practical with small groups, thereby enabling teachers to accurately diagnose learners' enabling skills. (See pages 275-277 for ways of enhancing control of all nine events of instruction in the small group.)

    f) A small group format permits students to initiate and/or respond to remarks or questions of the teacher or to those of other students, hence the term, "interactive communication."

    g) Attitude and problem solving (higher-order rule learning).

    h) Problems that have multiple solutions and an attitudinal component, and those that capture the students' interest and stimulate emotional involvement on the part of learners.

    i) Lectures can provide most of the events of instruction effectively in a probabilistic sense. However, it is difficult to adapt instruction to individual differences in a large group setting. The biggest limitations of the lecture by itself are a) achieving adequate control over the recall of prerequisite learnings and b) eliciting students' performance.

    j) (1) stimulating recall of prerequisites   (3) enhancing retention and transfer
        (2) providing learning guidance   (4) eliciting performance

    k) Since only a few learners can be called upon to respond, some will be neglected while others will be bored by questions and corrective feedback for others that is unnecessary for them. Providing all events effectively for individual learners is virtually impossible.

    l) Objectives are usually grouped for two-week units of study. Following the teaching of a unit using traditional large group methods, mastery (objective-referenced) tests are administered. Learners who show mastery proceed to self-instructional enrichment activities. Learners who do not exhibit mastery receive additional instruction via individual tutoring, small-group instruction or self study. These students are then retested; most will now achieve mastery.

By applying diagnostic progress testing and feedback with correction, instructional precision is enhanced and learning is improved for more students.

m) There is an increase in achievement of one standard deviation with mastery learning and of two standard deviations with tutoring. Dramatic improvements in large group instruction have also been achieved by supplementing the general mastery learning procedures with techniques that a) effectively stimulate recall of prerequisites, b) require student participation as part of learning guidance, and c) efficiently enhance retention (especially by means of suitable elaboration strategies).

Criteria for Evaluating the Application Exercise:

1. Will the suggested revisions effectively achieve desired events of instruction?

2. Is the suggested lesson adaptation appropriate for the group instructional setting?

3. Do the changes to the lesson capitalize on the instructional opportunities associated with small group instruction?

Sample answer for the application exercise requiring a revision of the lesson presented in workbook exercise 3a, Chapter 10.

a) Have students gather around you. Tell students that it's time for fun and then display a clock with movable hands that students can manipulate.

b) Review hour and half-hour briefly through your demonstration with clock. Have students come up and correct your planned mistakes and arrange for each student to respond verbally.

c) Continue this review by giving each student the chance to come up and use the clock to show his or her bedtime to the nearest half-hour.

d) Have students count by 5's in unison and monitor carefully their responses.

e) Then quickly quiz students, orally moving from one student to the next. For example, ask, when counting by 5's, what comes after 20, before 45, after 30, before 15, etc.

f) Demonstrate position of small hand for 5, 10, 15, 20 and 25 minutes before and after the hour. Select students one at a time to use the demonstration clock to represent these times by positioning the clock hands.

g) Treat 5-minute intervals 30-55 in the same manner and vary the hour.

h) Distribute a cardboard clock to each student. Have them practice as teacher calls out different times. Teacher monitors and gives feedback.

i) Give worksheet showing clock faces with times drawn on the faces. Students are to write the times shown. On the same worksheet is another section that only gives a blank clock face and a time in writing (__minutes after/before __ o'clock). Students are to draw the hands in their proper position. Corrective feedback is given as soon as students complete a section.

Lesson segments 'j' and 'k' would remain the same as in the original lesson.

INDIVIDUALIZED INSTRUCTION

Overview:

The intent of this chapter is to provide you with an understanding of various approaches to individualized instruction, the major advantages of such approaches, and the application of the events of instruction to individualized instruction. Consequently, the major emphasis is on verbal information as the cognitive component of a positive attitude toward using individualized methods in a systematic way.

Objectives:

1. When asked, in the form of an oral or written question, state:

    a)   the five purposes of delivery systems for individualized instruction.

    b)   the effects of individualized instruction upon the implementation of each of the events of instruction.

    c)   the five varieties of individualized instruction.

    d)   the major characteristics of materials used for individualized instruction.

    e)   the four components of an individualized module.

    f)   four advantages of individualized instruction over conventional instruction.

    g)   three examples of new technology most appropriate for individualized instruction.

  2) **When given descriptions of instruction, classify** the five varieties of individualized instruction by labeling examples of each variety.

Practice Exercises:

1. a) List the five broad purposes of individualized delivery systems.

      (1)

      (2)

      (3)

      (4)

      (5)

b)   How does individualized instruction affect application of the events of instruction? List the effects for each event.

   (1) Provide for Attention and Motivation

   (2) Present the Objective

   (3) Recall prerequisites

   (4) Present Stimulus

   (5) Provide Learning Guidance

   (6) Elicit Performance

   (7) Provide Feedback

   (8) Assess Performance

   (9) Enhance Retention and Transfer

c)   List five varieties of individualized instruction.

   (1)

   (2)

   (3)

   (4)

   (5)

d) Outline the major characteristics of materials used for individualized instruction.

e)   List the four components usually found in individualized modules.

   (1)

   (2)

   (3)

   (4)

f)   Many educators feel that individualized instruction is superior to conventional methods. List four characteristics of individualized instruction which most teachers would consider advantages.

   (1)

   (2)

   (3)

   (4)

g)   Give three examples of new technology appropriate for use in individualized instruction.

   (1)

   (2)

   (3)

2. Column A contains descriptions of different instructional settings. Column B contains varieties of individualized instruction. Match the type of instruction with the description by writing the letter from column B on the line to the left of each description in column A. Each response from column B may be used once, more than once, or not at all.

Column A

_____1. A graduate student produces an evaluation report on the effectiveness of a workshop as part of a course on adult learners.

_____2. A trainer asks shop foremen to assist in the design of a course by allowing them to select objectives and resources which will strengthen their individual supervisory skills.

_____3. A student prepares for a comprehensive examination in educational administration.

_____4. Kindergarten children visit the fire station as part of a teacher's plan for the study of community resources.

_____5. An advanced history class is given specific objectives and a resource list. Students may use any resources to accomplish the objectives.

_____6. At the completion of an assigned task, students may choose from a variety of activities at the science center.

_____7. Biology 105 students are to master common objectives in five modules. They take the test for each module only when they feel they have mastered the content.

Column B

a. Independent study

b. Learner-centered

c. Self-directed

d. Self-pacing

e. Student-determined

f. None of the above

Application Exercise:

Locate an individualized instruction module (may be CAI). Evaluate the module in terms of the events of instruction. Note which elements of the module meet the events. Evaluate as well for the external conditions of learning for the type(s) of learning covered in the module.

Feedback for Practice Exercises:

1. a) Assessing the entry skills of students; finding a starting point for each student; alternative materials and media; self-pacing of learning; progress checks.

   b) (1) Gaining attention...fewer problems; high student motivation based on success; easy to maintain
      (2) Informing of objective...highly structured nature makes the objective evident
      (3) Stimulating recall...easily achieved through careful sequencing; starting point for each student clearly assessed
      (4) Stimulus materials...carefully selected to match the learning
      (5) Learning guidance...prompts, cues, and suggestions used very precisely; carefully designed instruction
      (6) Eliciting performance/feedback...precisely managed in a built-in cycle; a strong feature of the materials
      (7) Assessment...used more often to check progress; often self-testing
      (8) Retention and transfer...accomplished in small groups or special projects matched to interests

   c) Independent study; self-directed; learner-centered; self-pacing; student-determined.

   d) More distinctly self-instructional; events of instruction and conditions of learning designed into the materials; materials perform the direct teaching; use alternative media and materials.

   e) Performance objective; materials and learning activities; self-evaluation method; teacher verification process.

   f) More frequent feedback; more frequent progress checks; more freedom of choice for learners; self-pacing.

   g) Microcomputers; video technology/interactive video/videodisk; information retrieval systems.

2. (1) a   (5) c
   (2) e   (6) b
   (3) a   (7) d
   (4) f

Criteria for Evaluating the application Exercise:

1. Is the content correctly categorized by type of learning?

2. Are the external conditions correctly listed for the type of learning?

3. Are illustrations of the application of the conditions of learning in the module accurate?

4. Are all the events of instruction accounted for by noting omissions and indicating appropriate conclusions?

Example of an answer for the application exercise:

Module Title: Designing Effective Forms

A. Content: Recognizing forms (DC)
Reasons for naming and numbering forms (VI)
Five zones of a form (VI, DC)
Naming forms (RU)
Self-instruction procedures (RU)
Captions and lines (DC, RU)
Box design (VI, DC, RU)

B. Evaluation of the Module

    1. External Conditions
       a) Defined concepts -   All conditions present but a larger variety of examples might be appropriate

       b) Rules -   Insufficient opportunity for learners to practice the rules

       c) Verbal information -   No opportunity to rehearse (practice) the information. Meaningful context appropriate

    2. Events of Instruction
       a) Gaining attention
       Comparison made between good tools and good forms -- improved performance with improved quality of tools
       b) Informing learners of objective
       List of objectives included in the module
       c) Stimulating recall of prior learning
       Concepts covered in earlier modules reviewed briefly at the beginning of this module
       d) Presenting the stimulus material
       Samples of forms and parts of forms used at key points in the module
       e) Providing learning guidance
       Written text is conversational and easy to read
       f) Eliciting performance
       Practice items followed each segment of instructions
       g) Providing feedback
       Answers given for practice items. Reasons for answers included
       h) Assessing performance
       Post-test measured performance. Multiple items used where appropriate
       i) Enhancing retention and transfer
       Summary of main principles given at the end of the module. No indication of transfer given but other modules follow.

    3. Overall   A good module. Layout could be improved to avoid crowding but events and conditions applied reasonably well with the exceptions noted above

EVALUATING INSTRUCTION

Overview:

One of the central components of many instructional systems is a feedback mechanism which evaluates the effectiveness or worth of the instruction or program. Chapter 16 considers two different evaluation models: Context-Input-Process-Product (CIPP), and goal-free evaluation.

Related loosely to these models is the dichotomy of formative and summative evaluation. This chapter introduces you to a three-stage model of formative evaluation (one-on-one, small-group and large-group). In considering these stages you should determine the feasibility or effectiveness of the instruction or instructional program. At the same time, consider how summative evaluation differs from formative evaluation.

Educational program evaluation studies investigate aptitude, support, and process variables. All may have important influences on the outcomes of instruction. Thus, these variables must be controlled for. How well these variables are controlled for has a major effect on the quality of evaluation activities.

Objectives:

1. When asked, in the form of an oral or written question, state:

    a) three critical questions that should be answered in evaluating of a lesson, course, topic, or instructional system.

    b) in your own words, definitions of the following terms:
        (1) educational evaluation
        (2) goal-free evaluation
        (3) CIPP model

    c) the differences between Stufflebeam's view of formative and summative evaluation.

    d) the major difference in emphasis between Scriven's goal-free and Stufflebeam's evaluation models.

    e) the importance of feasibility and effectiveness and their effect on the resultant instructional materials.

    f) the type of information gained from the following stages of formative evaluation: (1) one-to-one; (2) small-group; (3) field trial.

    g) the main question that is answered by summative evaluation.

    h) the function of randomization in evaluation.

  2. **Given descriptions of situations, classify** outcome, process, support, or aptitude variables by labeling each situation.

3. **Assuming the purpose of an evaluation is to find out if the objectives have been met, generate**, in writing, an appropriate technique for controlling for aptitude, support, and process variables.

4. **Assuming the purpose of an evaluation is to find out if the new program is better than the one it is intended to supplant, generate**, in writing, an appropriate technique for controlling for aptitude, support, and process variables.

5. **Assuming the purpose of an evaluation is to find out what additional effects a new program produces, generate**, in writing, an appropriate technique for controlling for aptitude, support, and process variables.

Practice Exercises:

1. a) What critical questions should be answered in evaluating a lesson, topic, course or instructional system?

    b) (1) What is educational evaluation? Define it in your own words.

        (2) Describe the meaning of goal-free evaluation.

        (3) Define the four elements of the CIPP evaluation model.

        _____

        _____

        _____

        _____

c) How does Stufflebeam's view of formative evaluation contrast with his view of summative evaluation?

d) What is the major difference in emphasis between Scriven's goal-free evaluation model and Stufflebeam's CIPP model?

e) Discuss the importance of feasibility and effectiveness in formative evaluation and their effect on the resultant instructional materials.

f) Briefly discuss the type of information obtained from the following stages of formative evaluation:
(1) one-to-one

(2) small-group

(3) field trial.

g) What is the main kind of decision for which evidence of summative evaluation is useful?

h) Describe the purpose that randomization serves in evaluation.

2. Classify each of the variables below as one of the following:
   (o) outcome
   (p) process
   (s) support
   (a) aptitude

   _____ home conditions

   _____ standardized test scores for IQ

   _____ level of formal education of instructor

   _____ instructor's judgment regarding the appropriateness
               of lesson for learners of differing abilities

   _____ quality of school facilities

   _____ scores on an arithmetic test at the end of instruction

   _____ reading readiness score

   _____ community environment

   _____ noise level of classroom

   _____ end-of-lesson reading achievement test scores

   _____ instructor's teaching experience

_____ range of learners' socioeconomic status

_____ English language fluency of instructor

_____ availability of reading materials in students' homes

3. Assume the purpose of the evaluation is to find out if the objectives of instruction have been met. How would you show that you have controlled for the following types of variables? (Exclude random selection.)

   a) aptitude

   b) support

   c) process

4. Assume the purpose of the evaluation is to find out if a new program is better than the one it is intended to replace. How would you show that you have controlled for the following types of variables? (Exclude random selection.)

   a) aptitude

   b) support

   c) process

5. Assume the purpose of the evaluation is to find out what additional effects a new program produces. How would you show that you have controlled for the following types of variables? (Exclude random selection.)

a) aptitude

b) support

c) process

Application Exercise:

1. Generate a written formative evaluation plan for an instructional module you have developed. Your plan should consider three stages of formative evaluation: one-to-one, small group, and field trial. Your plan should consider revising materials based on the one-to-one evaluations before conducting the small group evaluation -- likewise for the field trial phase. Your plan should also include a sequential description of the process, instruments, and data to be collected, and a rationale for collecting particular data.

2. State how you would consider Context, Input, Process and Product variables in the summative evaluation of your module.

Feedback for Practice Exercises:

1. a) Three critical questions that should be answered in evaluating a lesson, topic, course, or instructional system are:
   (1) Have the objectives been met?
   (2) Is it better than the unit it will supplant?
   (3) What additional effects does the new program produce?

   b) (1) Educational evaluation is, in a general sense, the assessment of the worth of many different aspects of educational products, proposals, systems, and institutions.

   (2) In applying goal-free evaluation, the evaluator examines the actual effects of an educational innovation and assesses the worth of these effects, whatever they may be. The intent, according to Scriven, is to document all effects in an effort to identify not only achievement of goals or objectives, but also to identify unintended outcomes, side effects, and secondary effects.

(3) The four elements of Stufflebeam's CIPP model may be described as follows.

    (a) Context evaluation formulates a rationale for determination of the system's objectives. This involves an analysis of the environment as well as needs and opportunities present.

    (b) Input evaluation provides information required for maximum utilization of resources in relation to goals. Concurrently, relevant strategies, capabilities, and implementation procedures are identified.

    (c) Process evaluation provides adequate feedback to the appropriate individuals. This may include a procedural record, existing and potential defects, and information necessary to make decisions.

    (d) Product evaluation offers an assessment of the extent to which desired ends are being attained. Generally, this is made by measuring and interpreting the attained effects of change.

c) Stufflebeam sees formative evaluation as serving the needs of decision making about program development. Summative evaluation, in contrast, is viewed as a basis for accountability.

d) The major emphasis in Stufflebeam's model is "continuous planning". Scriven emphasizes "verified performance."

e) The practical feasibility of the lesson under evaluation is an important formative consideration for revision efforts. Likewise, the effectiveness with which an instructional innovation meets its objectives is an essential purpose of formative evaluation. The revised form of the instructional program should be molded from evidence, regarding both feasibility and effectiveness, collected and interpreted during formative evaluation.

f) Some of the information which may be obtained from the different stages of formative evaluation is indicated below. It should be noted, however, that much overlap in the types of information obtained exists among different stages. In addition, other types of data may be quite useful for specific evaluative efforts.

    (1) One-to-one evaluation:
        (a) errors in estimating students' entry behaviors
        (b) unclear presentation
        (c) unclear test questions or directions
        (d) inappropriate expectations of the outcomes of learning.

    (2) Small-group evaluation:
        (a) when and how much learning occurs based on pretest, embedded, and post-test scores
        (b) unclear presentation
        (c) test questions needing revision.

    (3) Field trial:
        (a) feasibility of use

      (b) effectiveness of instruction
      (c) student and instructor attitudes
      (d) student and instructor behavior
      (e) test scores indicating gains in achievement.

g)   Summative evaluation is useful for deciding whether a new unit is better than the one it has replaced and should therefore be adopted for continued use.

h)   Randomization is the best overall way to control for variables in an evaluation study. When a sufficient number of students can be assigned to control or experimental groups in a truly random manner, the effects of nontreatment variables can be assumed to occur in a random fashion across all groups. An additional benefit of randomization is that other variables, whose potential influence was not anticipated or measured, are controlled for also.

2. The appropriate classification for each evaluation variable is indicated next to the left of the variable.

SUPPORT	home conditions
APTITUDE	standardized test scores for IQ
SUPPORT	level of formal education of instructor
PROCESS	instructor's judgment regarding the appropriateness of lesson for learners of differing abilities
SUPPORT	quality of school facilities
OUTCOME	scores on an arithmetic test at the end of instruction
APTITUDE	reading readiness score
SUPPORT	community environment
SUPPORT	noise level of classroom
OUTCOME	end-of-lesson reading achievement test scores
SUPPORT	instructor's teaching experience
APTITUDE	range of learners' socioeconomic status
PROCESS	English language fluency of instructor
SUPPORT	availability of reading materials in students' homes

3. Assuming the purpose of the evaluation is to find out if the objectives of instruction have been met, you could show that you have controlled for evaluation variables in some of the ways mentioned below.

   a) aptitude --
      (1) State the level of intelligence of the students receiving instruction. This is often done by reporting students' mean scores and standard deviations on a standard test for intelligence.
      (2) Report correlated measures, such as socioeconomic status or learners' previous grade point average.

   b) support --
      (1) Report which measures of support you used (e.g., judgments of the quality of the school facilities where the evaluations took place) and the outcomes of these measures. These could be presented in a manner which shows their possible influence on instructional outcomes.
      (2) Indicate the English language fluency of the learners and the communities from which they come.

   c) process --
      (1) Show the effects of different presentation styles in the instructional situation.
      (2) Present anecdotal or survey data regarding the facilitator's attitude toward the instructional innovation.
      (3) Indicate the English language fluency of each of the instructors.

4. Assuming the purpose of the evaluation is to find out if a new program is better than one it is intended to supplant, you could show that you have controlled for evaluation variables in some of the ways mentioned below.

   a) aptitude --
      (1) Compare the outcomes of aptitude measures for students in the new program and similar students in the same school who are in a program being compared to the new program.
      (2) Present the findings of statistical analyses which "partial out" the effects of aptitude variables.

   b) support --
      (1) Demonstrate the equivalence among subjects, classes, or schools being compared.
      (2) Provide qualitative or quantitative data about the environment.

   c) process --
      (1) You could report any differences in process which exist between the new instructional program and other programs, particularly any which are being used or are also being considered for adoption.
      (2) Provide evidence of equivalence in the way the compared instruction is delivered.

5. Assuming the purpose of the evaluation is to find out what additional effects a program produces, you could show that you have controlled for evaluation variables in some of the ways mentioned below.

  a) aptitude --
    (1) Present the findings of statistical analyses which "partial out" the effects of aptitude variables.

  b) support --
    (1) Provide descriptive evidence that shows the new program was run in an equivalent environment to the old one.

  c) process --
    (1) Present evidence that students' attitudes were not greatly affected by factors extraneous to the program, such as charismatic human models.
    (2) Show that the new program was equivalent in process with the old program.

Criteria for Evaluating the Application Exercise:

1. The formative evaluation plan indicates solid evidence that the stated instructional objectives (learning outcomes) will be met.

2. The evaluation plan indicates what effect the evidence gathered will have on revising the draft instructional materials.

3. The issues of feasibility and effectiveness are addressed.

4. The instruments used to conduct the formative evaluation are discussed in detail.

5. Rationales for the formative evaluation instruments are clear.

6. There is an adequate description of the participants and processes involved with all stages of formative evaluation.

7. The outcomes (data) of formative evaluation activities are summarized in a clear, usable fashion.

8. The evaluation plan indicates how aptitude, support, and process variables will be controlled for.

9. Revision processes based on summarized evaluation data are proposed.

Example of a formative evaluation plan by Greg Stevens

Plan for conducting a formative evaluation

The module I will be evaluating is on the topic of resumé preparation, and is designed for upper-division college students. The module should take approximately one hour.

My first step will be to conduct one-to-one evaluations. This step is designed to test the validity of the objectives and the accuracy and clarity of the materials and test items. The first way to assess this will be to give the completed materials to a subject matter expert. This person is an expert in resumé preparation, and will review the materials and provide comments as to the validity of the objectives, and perceived clarity of the materials and test items. The SME's comments will be collected from a structured questionnaire.

The second step of the one-to-one evaluation will be to have learners from my target audience work through the materials. I will sit down with three students as they work through the materials. Each student will be asked to provide comments as he or she works through the module. Additionally, I will ask the learner questions about the clarity of the materials as they work through them. Upon completion of the module, I will have each learner complete a post-test and an attitude questionnaire which assesses feelings toward the instruction. I would then review the data gathered from the SME and from the three learners (comments, performance, and attitude), for the purpose of determining if and where the module might be revised in order to make it more effective.

After the revisions based on the one-on-one evaluations have been made I would perform a small-group evaluation. In addition to continuing to collect data regarding the clarity of the materials and the learners' attitudes toward the instruction, I would also gather data about how much the module was teaching. To accomplish this, a small group of 8 students would be assembled, and each given a copy of the module. Before beginning the module each student will be tested, using a pretest, to determine his or her entry skills, and what he or she knows about the terminal objective. Both the pretest and the post-test will have items for every subordinate objective to detect entry and learned skills. An attitude questionnaire will be used to determine student interest and enjoyment of the materials. The data collected from these instruments will be reviewed and necessary revisions to the materials will be made.

My last step would be to conduct a field trial. This would examine the effects of the module in a setting representative of the target setting in which the instruction is to be implemented. In this case, two sections of a job-search seminar conducted by the Florida State University Career Center will be used. Data collected from this evaluation will include student performance and attitude data. I would also collect attitude data from instructors using the module. The student attitude questionnaire would be the same one used in the small group evaluation.

The instructor questionnaire will assess such areas as ease of use, and perceived effectiveness. Increases of learning will be analyzed objective-by-objective from the pre and post-test. Additionally, I would observe the implementation to assess instructor student interaction, and possible problems with using the module in a self-study format. This data will be assessed to determine if the module is both feasible and effective. Problems with either of these two areas will result in the need to revise the materials before they are implemented full-scale.